BRETTON WOODS INSTITUTIONS & NEOLIBERALISM

Historical Critique of Policies, Structures, & Governance

of the International Monetary Fund & the World Bank,

with Case Studies

MARK J. WOLFF, J.D., LL.M. (in Tax Law)

Professor of Law
Saint Thomas University School of Law
Miami Gardens, Florida, USA

PACEM IN TERRIS PRESS

www.paceminterrispress.com

2018

An earlier version of the material in this book
was previously published as:
Wolff, Mark J. (2013), "Failure of the International Monetary Fund & World Bank
to Achieve Integral Development: A Critical Historical Assessment of
Bretton Woods Institutions' Policies, Structure & Governance,"
Syracuse Journal of International Law and Commerce: Vol. 41: No. 1, Article 4
(available at: https://surface.syr.edu?jilc/vol41/iss1/4)

ISBN-13: 978-0999608852
ISBN-10: 0999608851

Cover photo is of Mount Washington Hotel
in Bretton Woods, New Hampshire, which was the site of the 1944
United Nations Monetary and Financial Conference ("Bretton Woods Conference").
(Cover photo from Shutterstock.)

Pacem in Terris Press
is sponsored by:

PAX ROMANA / CMICA-USA
1025 Connecticut Avenue NW, Suite 1000,
Washington DC 20036
www.paceminterris.net

PROFESSOR MARK J. WOLFF received his B.A. *magna cum laude* from Wadhams Hall Seminary-College, his J.D. *magna cum laude* from Nova Southeastern University School of Law, and his LL.M. (in Taxation) from New York University Graduate School of Law. He is admitted to the Florida Bar, Southern District Court of Florida, the Fifth and Eleventh Circuit Courts of Appeals, Supreme Court of Florida, United States Tax Court, and Supreme Court of the United States.

After being engaged in the private practice of tax, corporate and securities law for almost a decade, he was appointed in 1984 as a founding faculty member and Assistant Dean at St. Thomas University School of Law in Miami, Florida. Professor Wolff now enjoys the rank of tenured full Professor of Law, and over the past thirty-four academic years has specialized in teaching courses in various areas of Federal Income Taxation, Federal Estate and Gift Taxation, Estate Planning, Comparative International Taxation, Tax Policy, Agency and Partnership, and Business Associations, Corporate Taxation, and Contracts, as well as Advanced Jurisprudence Seminars. As a professor at Saint Thomas University School of Law he was the recipient of the University-wide John Cardinal Newman Award for Excellence in Teaching.

In the domestic arena, Professor Wolff was elected to public office in 1987, serving as Vice Mayor and Commissioner for the City of Coral Gables. During his elected tenure, he served as Chairman of the Municipal Finance and Taxation Committee for the Florida League of Cities, Member of the Finance Administration and Inter-Governmental Affairs Committee of the National League of Cities, and on the Board of Directors and as Treasurer of the Miami-Dade County League of Cities, and as Vice Chair and on the Executive Committee of the Board of Trustees of Wadhams Hall Seminary-College.

He is currently Executive Director of the Miami-Dade County Educational Facilities Authority. During Professor Wolff's tenure, the Authority has issued in excess of 2.5 billion in tax exempt bonds for educational institutions of higher learning, and never experienced a single default. He is also Legal Counsel and Board Member, Malta Projects of Southeastern Florida, Inc., an affiliate of the American Association of the Sovereign Military Hospitaller Order of Saint John of Jerusalem of Rhodes and of Malta, as well as General Counsel and a member of the Board of Directors of Pax Romana-USA, a member of the Board of Directors of the Human Rights Institute at St. Thomas University, and he serves on the Faculty Advisory Board for the Center for Ethics at St. Thomas University.

In the international arena, Professor Wolff formerly served as an International Vice President of Pax Romana / International Catholic Movement for Intellectual and Cultural Affairs and as Main Representative of Pax Romana at United Nations Headquarters in New York City. He also founded, and is Director of, the St. Thomas University School of Law United Nations Externship Program at United Nations Headquarter in New York City. The program involves numerous St. Thomas law students credentialed by permanent missions, inter-governmental organizations and non-governmental organizations as representatives to United Nations Headquarters in New York and Geneva.

Currently, he serves as an Adviser to the Permanent Mission of the Order of Malta to the United Nations Headquarters in New York. In addition, he has served as a member of, and the head of delegations, on behalf of the Sovereign Military Hospitaller Order of Saint John of Jerusalem of Rhodes and of Malta at United Nations World Conferences and International Consultative Conferences, and he has addressed the plenary sessions of these Conferences and the General Assembly of the United Nations.

I would like to express appreciation to the following persons
for their support and assistance:
Ambassador Extraordinary & Plenipotentiary Permanent Observer
at the United Nations Oscar de Rojas;
Emeritus Professor of Philosophy & Religion
at St. Thomas University Edward "Joe" Holland,
especially for his excellent editing and patience;
and to my research assistants
Cesar Baldelomar, Ansell Fernandez,
Victor Gabuardi, David Hernandez,
Candice C. Izaguirre, and Daniel Joseph.
Any errors are my responsibility.

TABLE OF CONTENTS

FORWARD

Edward "Joe" Holland, Ph.D.

President, Pax Romana / CMICA-USA

I t is indeed an honor for Pacem in Terris Press, sponsored by Pax Romana / Catholic Movement for Intellectual & Cultural Affairs USA, to publish this important and insightful book by Professor Mark J. Wolff on the Bretton Woods Institutions in relation to Neoliberalism.

Background to
Professor Wolff's Important Book

The book is a product of Professor Wolff's extensive research and rich practical experience at the United Nations in New York City. There, he served for many years as the Main Representative of Pax Romana in its consultative relationship with the United Nations Economic and Social Council.

Professor Wolff also worked closely with, and still works closely with, the Permanent Observer Mission of the Sovereign Military Order of Malta to the United Nations, as well as with the Permanent Observer Mission of the Holy See to the United Nations. In addition, he has participated in many important United Nations global conferences, and he has addressed the United Nations General Assembly.

But the most important source for Professor Wolff's research and experience shared in this book has been his founding and directing, over several decades, the Pax Romana / St. Thomas University School of Law Internship at the United Nations in New York City.

During those decades, and still today, Professor Wolff, every semester and for summer sessions, places intelligent and devoted third-year law students as legal staff with United Nations offices and with inter-governmental and national missions to the United Nations, as well as with offices of NGO representations to the United Nations. Law students completing their internship at the United Nations typically report that the experience changed their lives.

Those law students' experience and Professor Wolff's care-filled mentoring of them has provided him with enormous and invaluable insight into the great global issues and contentious global policy debates addressed by the United Nations and faced by our global human family.

Professor Wolff is also an experienced elected political official and an attorney specializing in tax law, as well as someone still active in the field of public finance. Within United Nations context, therefore, he has taken a special interest in the International Financial Institutions, as they have attempted to govern the emerging global economy. One valuable fruit of that special interest is this important and insightful book.

Professor Wolff's Inspiration by Catholic Social Teaching

Inspiring Professor Wolff's deep knowledge shared in this book, and also inspiring his public and professional life, has been his deep devotion to what is known as "Catholic Social Teaching."

That ethical wisdom tradition, with roots in the Hebrew and Christian scriptures, has also drawn on the philosophical wisdom traditions of Aristotle, the Roman Stoics, and Saint Thomas Aquinas. In addition, in

2

the era of globalization, it is now learning from other philosophical and religious wisdom traditions across our global human family.

Many years ago, Michel Camdessus, at the time Managing Director and Chairperson of the Executive Board of the International Monetary Fund and himself long drawn to Catholic Social Teaching, published a collection of his addresses under the title *From Recovery to Crisis* (International Monetary Fund, 1999). In the Forward to that publication, he described the global economy as a "system in crisis" (p. v).

In response, Monsieur Camdessus called for "strengthening the international financial architecture," especially through "public and private transparency," "international standards for securities," and "supervision of financial institutions" (p. vi). "Strengthening" in those areas, he judged, would assist the global financial community to facilitate an "orderly process" of global financial integration through the "orderly liberalization of capital movement."

Unfortunately, during those same years and still today, what has emerged instead is what we now know as the libertarian doctrine of "Neoliberalism, " which I will name here "Neoliberal Libertarianism."

It is the impact of Neoliberal Libertarianism, condemned by Catholic Social Teaching,[1] on the Bretton Woods institutions and specifically on the International Monetary Fund and World Bank, that Professor Wolff so critically and so insightfully addresses in his book. I hope that all readers of Professor Wolff's important book will be as grateful as I am for his critical and insightful contributions.

---

[1] Pacem in Terris Press is also proud to have published a vigorous critique, informed by Catholic Social Teaching, of the principal theoretic foundation for Neoliberal Libertarianism, namely the so-called 'Austrian school' of Economics. The book was written by Angus Sibley, now retired from the London Stock Exchange and presently living in Paris. His challenging book is titled *The "Poisoned Spring" of Economic Libertarianism* (Pacem in Terris Press, 2011). In that title, the phrase " Poisoned Spring" is taken from the 1931 encyclical letter by Pope Pius XI, *Quadragesimo Anno*, which boldly condemned economic libertarianism – now repackaged as "Neoliberalism."

PREFACE

Ambassador Oscar R. de Rojas

Permanent Observer of the Sovereign Military Order of Malta
to the United Nations

T hrough this book, Professor Mark Wolff has rekindled an interest in one of the most controversial –and certainly most important— issues of our times: How to best govern this ever increasingly interdependent, globalized, hyper-connected, complex and, yes, dangerous world.

Many people shudder at any implication of supra-national authorities for "governing the world", but we use the term here not so much in relation to actual governing, but to that of *governance*. The two words are similar, but they mean something quite different. Governance refers to the set of international structures, institutions and mechanisms that humankind has put in place in order to pursue the global common good and help the world avoid as much as possible wars, crises and calamities of all types. Good examples of those institutions are the United Nations, NATO, and, indeed, the Bretton Woods institutions, which are the specific focus of this book.

Good governance has always been considered one of the key variables to make any human group perform effectively. Good governance is needed (though sometimes taken for granted) at the family, community, national, regional and international levels. The Bretton Woods institutions (BWI) operate of course at the global level, and it is there that this book tries to analyze if the conditions of good governance have been effectively in place, in the World Bank and the International Monetary Fund, since 1944. And it is not only important to see if the BWI have promoted good governance within the countries that they are meant to serve, but also is they have applied the principles of good governance to their own internal functioning, structures, rules and procedures.

Professor Wolff makes a solid argument for an overall negative verdict, especially on this last aspect. The Bretton Woods are *not* (and were never designed to be) democratic institutions. The BWI follow essentially same rules of private-sector financial entities: basically, that it is the number of shares owned by a particular person/country that determines the voting and decision-making power. Clearly, rich developed countries, who promoted the creation of the BWI to begin with, have been the ones with the most votes and the most power. This has led to a design and evolution of the institutions along the lines of what those developed countries considered the "optimal" economic and financial models - especially in furthering their own economic interests.

As Professor Wolff clearly points out, this has meant, in practical terms, that poorer, developing countries have had little choice but to accept policy "conditions" in order to benefit from IMF structural adjustment programs and receive loans from the World Bank. What have been those conditions? Essentially, that countries follow policies falling within the prevailing neo-liberal economic paradigm (what in the 1980s came to be known as the "Washington Consensus"), including in particular trade liberalization, economic deregulation, and privatization strategies.

The results, especially in the last decades of the 20th century and beginning of the 21st, were often disastrous. Many countries, after applying those policies, saw themselves thrown into situations of economic stagnation and dependency, with rising unemployment, inequality, poverty and unrest. Ironically (or one could say, hypocritically), countries who espoused with great fanfare neoliberal policies did not apply them within their own borders! A perfect example of this is the "bailouts" and regulations undertaken in the United States following the financial crisis of 2008.

Developing countries have for decades been clamoring for a change in the rules of the game, for an improvement of global economic and financial governance so as to make the corresponding structures and institutions more just, equitable and development-friendly. These are often called "systemic issues." because they deal with the way the international financial, monetary and trade systems operate, individually and in conjunction with each other. As can be imagined, there has been great resistance on the part of the richer countries to introduce any changes in the system that do not conform to their interests and priorities and to their political ideology and objectives.

Given the little power developing countries have had in changing things "from the inside" in the Bretton Woods institutions themselves (and here we normally also include the World Trade Organization, WTO), their preferred forum for action has been the United Nations, where each country can have its voice heard and where, by banding together (in groupings such as the "Group of 77" and the Non-Aligned Movement), their actions could be made more effective.

Initiatives thus began to be taken by developing countries in the mid-1970s, with the proposal to establish a "New International Economic Order." Discussions and negotiations dragged on for years, only to collapse at the failure to come to an agreement precisely on how to deal with the "systemic issues." The industrial countries rejected the notion that those issues could be considered in the United Nations, insisting that the only proper venues to do so were the BWI/WTO themselves.

The process received a new breath of momentum with the arrival of the new millennium and the adoption of the Millennium Development

Goals (MDG). Many pointed out that it would be impossible to reach the MDG if the amount of resources available to developing countries did not increase considerably, both from domestic and international sources.

This in turn led to the renewal of the question of the "development friendliness" of the international economic, financial and trading *systems:* If significant changes were not carried out in these, to support the efforts to increase the flow of resources to countries, then the whole exercise would be doomed to fail.

Thus, arose the initiative called "Financing for Development" (FfD), which consisted of having an in-depth, integrated discussion of *all* the variables that impact development, *including* the systemic ones. The process of preparation of the FfD Conference, as it eventually came to be called, was painstakingly arduous and slow – some called it a "mission impossible."

It took three years just to agree on the agenda and the official name of the conference! Finally, a deal was struck whereby developing countries accepted, for the first time, to discuss improving *domestic* governance within their own countries, and developed countries agreed to include a final agenda item entitled "increasing the coherence and consistency of the international financial, monetary and trade systems in support of development". An important part of this agreement was that the BWI and the WTO would be invited to participate with full voice and decision-making power in the conference (something the Group of 77 developing countries had resisted for years).

The International Conference on Financing for Development (later also called the Monterrey Conference), took place in Monterrey, Mexico, at the summit level, at the end of March 2002. It was hailed as an outstanding success.

The document adopted by the participating heads of state and government – called the "Monterrey Consensus"— contained six sections on what actions the international community needed to undertake collectively and in cooperation in order to facilitate the attainment of the MDG. These sections were: mobilizing domestic resources, increasing foreign private capital flows, increasing foreign aid, addressing debt problems, making international trade a true engine of development, and addressing the coherence and consistency of the international economic system – the famous systemic issues. (which implicitly, though not explicitly, included the reform of the functioning of the BWI and the WTO).

The first years after the Monterrey Conference were of considerable optimism, with a prevailing feeling that a watershed had been reached in dealing with the governance of the world economy. The BWI continued to be actively engaged in the follow-up process to the conference, and participation of other important stakeholders, such as the business sector and civil society, was also maintained.

But the process suffered from a fundamental deficiency: It lacked a "home." The crafters of the Monterrey Consensus had (perhaps deliberately) left out the establishment of an institutional, inter-govern-mental commission or other mechanism to carry out an effective follow-up to the conference, as had been done with other previous important UN conferences, such as those on the Environment, on Social Development, on Population, and on Women.

As those first few years passed, the momentum began to decrease and the entire FfD process to lose steam. Then came a stinging blow: The financial crisis of 2008. Rather than utilizing the FfD mechanism to address the crisis at the worldwide level, where all countries and institutions could participate (and especially taking into account that a second conference had already been convened to take place in Doha, Qatar, in December 2008), the most important developed countries decided to forego the UN route and deliberate on the crisis in a totally different forum.

They decided to use the "Group of 20", a group of so-called "systemically significant" countries that had already been in existence for some time, to make it the central point for dealing with the crisis at a global level. The United States convened a summit meeting of the G-20 in Washington in November of 2008, literally just weeks before the FfD conference in Doha was to take place.

From that point onwards, the old goal of using the universal, democratic United Nations forum as the central place to address issues of international economic development, cooperation and governance quickly began to unravel. All the years of patient effort were, again, essentially, lost.

The G-20 was enthroned as the new forum *par excellence* to discuss matters of global economic governance – notwithstanding, as Professor Wolff so eloquently points out, the fact that it is an elite, self-appointed group, lacking legitimacy, representation and accountability. Even though some key developing "emerging economy" countries are part of the G-20, it is still basically controlled by the Group of 8 established, developed countries. And, within this group, there is little appetite to change the rules of a game -including the BWI - that has worked well for them.

The question posed today is: Can the world economy of the 21st century continue to operate efficiently and equitably with institutions and structures that were set up in 1944? Will countries tolerate this? Will some other crisis be needed in order to replant the seeds of change? Professor Wolff's analysis goes a long way in helping us ponder these questions – and to hope that there will still come a new chance to establish a truly just and effective international economic order.

New York City,
October 2017

1

INTRODUCTION

I n July 1944, delegates from forty-four allied nations gathered at the Mount Washington Hotel in Bretton Woods, New Hampshire. The meeting resulted in the creation of the International Bank for Reconstruction and Development ("IBRD"), and the International Monetary Fund ("IMF"). The BWI encompass the World Bank and the IMF.[1] The World Bank actually refers to two banks: the International Bank for

---

[1] DEP'T OF STATE, PROCEEDINGS AND DOCUMENTS OF UNITED NATIONS MONETARY AND FINANCIAL CONFERENCE VOL. I at 5 (1948), https://fraser.stlouisfed.org/files/docs/publications/books/1948_state_bwood_v1.pdf. [hereinafter "Bretton Woods Conference Vol. I"]. The delegates gathered to create institutions that would regulate the international monetary system and reconstruct the international relations. *Id.* at 5-7. *See* LEE E. PRESTON & DUANE WINDSOR, THE RULES OF THE GAME IN THE GLOBAL ECONOMY: POLICY REGIMES FOR INTERNATIONAL BUSINESS 132–33 (Kluwer Academic Publishers, 2d. ed. 1997) (explaining that the IMF was established to carry out exchange, reserve, and short–term loan functions normally associated with "bank," while the IBRD is essentially a "Fund" for providing long–term loans). The purpose of these institutions was to stabilize the global economy and fund reconstruction of countries recovering from World War II. JOSEPH E. STIGLITZ, GLOBALIZATION AND ITS DISCONTENTS 12 (W. W. Norton & Company, 2003). *See* DEP'T OF PUBLIC INFO., EVERY-ONE'S UNITED NATIONS: A HANDBOOK ON THE UNITED NATIONS ITS STRUCTURE AND AC-TIVITIES 364–65 (United Nations Publications, 9th ed. 1979) (explaining that the IBRD was established to assist in the reconstruction and development of members' territories by facilitating the investment of capital for productive purposes; to promote private foreign investment and to supplement it by providing loans for productive purposes; and to promote growth of international trade and maintenance of equilibrium in balances of payments by encouraging international investment for the development of the productive sources of the Bank's members).

Reconstruction and Development and the International Development Association.[2]

The IMF was established with the purposes of facilitating international monetary cooperation; promoting exchange rate stability; assisting in the establishment of multilateral payment systems; eliminating foreign exchange restrictions; and providing loans to nations experiencing balance of payments issues--all for the purpose of creating conditions for strong economic growth.[3] The IMF created an orderly basis for international currency exchange, and established both stabilization and adjustment mechanisms.

However, scholars worldwide have clearly demonstrated the inability of the Bretton Woods Institutions ("BWI") to promote authentic sustainable development.[4]

Some have also criticized the BWI for their inability to rehabilitate, evolve, and reform their respective policies.[5] Some scholars argue that the core of this problem is the voting structures of the BWI.[6] Additional critiques address the lack of transparency and limited participation by developing countries in formulation of BWI' policies; both deficien-

---

[2] See About the World Bank, WORLD BANK, http://www.worldbank.org/en/about (last visited June 6, 2017). The World Bank Group refers to the two banks and three other agencies: the International Finance Corporation, the Multilateral Investment Guarantee Agency, and the International Centre for Settlement of Investment Disputes. Id.

[3] See DEP'T OF STATE, supra note 2, at 55.

[4] See infra Chapter I note 6; see infra Chapter II.E and accompanying text; see PRESTON & WINDSOR, infra note 2; see also EDWARD S. MASON & ROBERT E. ASHER, THE WORLD BANK SINCE BRETTON WOODS 21, 22 (1973). The IBRD provided loans to support reconstruction in war-damaged countries, and later promoted economic growth and development in nations with low per–capita income. See PRESTON & WINDSOR, infra note 2; see also MASON & ASHER, supra.

[5] What Are the Main Concerns and Criticisms about the World Bank and IMF?, BRETTON WOODS PROJECT (Aug. 23, 2005) ("[c]riticism of the World Bank and the IMF encompasses a whole range of issues but they generally center around concern about the approaches adopted by the World Bank and the IMF in formulating their policies, and the way they are governed."). "This includes the social and economic impact these policies have on the population of countries who avail themselves of financial assistance from these two institutions, and accountability for these impacts." Id.

[6] See infra Chapter II.E.

cies have resulted in fewer developing countries benefiting from these policies.[7]

Acknowledging these critiques, this book demonstrates that current BWI policies must be fundamentally redesigned, since many are archaic and others are counter-productive to integral sustainable development in the current global economy. Further, the book argues that the dominant nations in the BWI have forced their political agendas on the rest of the world while hiding behind the veil of these multilateral global financial institutions.[8]

In making these arguments, the book begins with a review of the origin, purpose, and structures of the BWI and offer a critique of their voting structures. Next, the book analyzes and critiques the neoliberal revival of the classical laissez-faire liberal ideology on a global scale, and it shows how it has played out in the Asian financial crisis, the current world financial crisis, and the on-going debt crisis. Five case studies are provided and discussed: the first on Argentina; the second on Sub-Saharan Africa; the third on the Asian Crisis; the fourth on Bangladesh; and the fifth on Ghana. The book then analyzes other institutions' alternative solutions to the ongoing problems with the BWI, specifically the Monterey Consensus, developed by the United Nations Financing for Development process, the "Heavily Indebted Poor Countries," created by the World Bank, and the G-20 [9], a policy-advising group of 20 countries claiming to represent the most "systemically significant" world economies. Finally, the conclusion summarizes the critique of the BWI and suggests alternative strategies.

Chapter 2 first reviews the events and global instability that led to the Bretton Woods Conference creating the early BWI, and then explains

---

[7] See infra Chapter II note 29 and accompanying text.
[8] See infra Chapter II note 64 and accompanying text.
[9] See Historical Overview, G20.ORG,
https://www.g20.org/Webs/G20/EN/G20/History/history_node.html (last visited June 06, 2017); see infra Chapter IV.C.

the Bretton Woods Conference itself and the global response to the creation of the BWI.[10] Chapter 2 concludes with a critical analysis of the IMF and World Bank voting structures.[11]

Chapter 3 begins by showing how neoliberal agendas influence the policies of the BWI through vote and governance.[12] A historical analysis of the rise of contemporary neoliberal ideology is provided.[13] At the heart of this has been the University of Chicago School of Economics, led by the late Professor Milton Friedman, and the Austrian School of Economics. Both schools were highly influential in developing a new and problematic model of so-called global 'development' for the BWI. The chapter then examines loan conditionality, that is, the mechanism by which the BWI pressure other countries into accepting neoliberal economic ideas and strategies.[14]

Chapter 4 provides a critical analysis of the neoliberal ideology in its application to the Asian Financial Crisis,[15] along with case studies showing its impact on Argentina, Sub-Saharan Africa, and Asia.[16]

Chapter 5 analyzes alternative solutions, which have been proposed by various global endeavors. It begins with an examination of the Monterrey Consensus, the product of an international conference held in Monterrey, Mexico.[17] Chapter 5 then examines The Heavily Indebted Poor Countries, a program created by the World Bank and the IMF, which currently classifies forty developing countries with high levels of

---

[10] *See infra* Chapter II.A–C.

[11] *See infra* Chapter II.D–E.

[12] *See infra* Chapter III.A.

[13] *See infra* Chapter III.B.

[14] *See infra* Chapter III.C.

[15] *See infra* Chapter III.D.3.

[16] *See infra* Chapter III.D.1–2.

[17] *See* Inaamul Haque & Ruxandra Burdescu, *Monterrey Consensus on Financing for Development: Response Sought from Economic Law*, 27 B.C. INT'L & COMP. L. REV. 219 (2004); *see infra* Chapter IV.A (stating the conference in Monterrey, Mexico comprised of over fifty Heads of State, two hundred Ministers of Finance, and the Heads of the United Nations, IMF, World Bank, and World Trade Organization).

poverty and debt, which are eligible for special assistance.[18] Further, the G-20 is a group of twenty countries that hold periodic meetings to review and promote discussions pertaining to the promotion of international financial stability and the governance of the world economy.[19]

The BWI have impeded authentic development. These institutions thus require fundamental reform, including overhauls to their policies, voting systems, and governance structures. Chapter 6 proposes alternative strategies for authentic sustainable development through other multilateral global institutions and concludes that the BWI, due to their lending policies and governing structures, have restrained authentic global development.

During the recent opening of the 72nd session of the General Assembly, the UN announced the creation of an accelerator to achieve the sustainable development goals by 2030.[20] "The new accelerator-like program will convene national and city leaders, businesses, financial institutions, and community development advocates to develop solutions for the SDGs–particularly energy, water, ecosystems restoration, food systems, sustainable cities, and a circular economy–that can scale and apply across national borders."[21] So far, the SDGs have moved Costa Rica to make great progress in renewal energy, India in smart sanitation,

---

[18] *See* Eric A. Friedman, *Debt Relief in 1999: Only One Step on a Long Journey*, 3 YALE HUM. RTS. & DEV. L.J. 191, 191–94 (2000); *see infra* Chapter IV.B.

[19] *See* Abdul Ruff, *G20 to Improve Trade Governance*, FOREIGN POLICY NEWS (July 15, 2016), http://foreignpolicynews.org/2016/07/15/g20-improve-trade-governance/ (providing that the group consists of both developed and developing countries, heads of state and government, finance ministers and central bank governors); *see infra* Chapter IV.C.

[20] *See* Eillie Anzilotti, *The UN Is Forming an Accelerator To Make Its Sustainable Development Goals A Reality*, FAST COMPANY, https://www.fastcompany.com/40471083/the-un-is-forming-an-accelerator-to-make-its-sustainable-development-goals-a-reality (last visited on Sept. 24, 2017) (announcing the launching of the Partnering for Green Growth and the Global Goals 2030 ("P4G") during the 72nd Session of the UN General Assembly); *Sustainable Development Goals*, UNITED NATIONS, *available at* http://www.un.org/sustainabledevelopment/sustainable-development-goals/ (last visited Sept. 21, 2017) (outlining the seventeen goals to be achieved by developing nations).

[21] *See* Anzilotti, *supra* note 20.

and Volvo in moving away from gas powered vehicles.[22] Business leaders within developing countries look at the SDGs as a great business opportunity; and are all too happy to see the United States backing out of the Paris Agreement and away from the great economic growth that was expected to be achieved as a result of meeting the SDGs.[23]

---

[22] *See id.*

[23] *See* Corinne Purtill, *The US is missing out on the biggest business opportunity of the future, and one of India's top executives is "delighted,"* QUARTZ MEDIA (last visited on Sept. 24, 2017), https://qz.com/1082930/anand-mahindra-sustainable-development-goals-are-biggest-business-opportunity-of-the-decade/ (providing an account of how the development goals are prime targets for companies in developing countries looking to expand their portfolios and increase their revenues).

BRETTON WOODS INSTITUTIONS

Worldwide Economic Instability
after World War I

A world trading system was practically nonexistent during the Great Depression because there were no major multilateral trading agreements or international agencies at the time to regulate or promote trade relations between countries.[1] Developed countries pursued nationalistic policies, such as closing their borders to imports, in an effort to protect their domestic productions and to shift unemployment to the nations from which they formerly imported.[2] At the mercy of their "European Masters,"[3] developing countries suffered from these isolationist policies, as they were cut off from their trading partners and no longer had external purchasers for their nationally produced goods.[4]

---

[1] *See* KENT ALBERT JONES, WHO'S AFRAID OF THE WTO? 68 (2004) (discussing how the world trading system after World War I collapsed during the Great Depression partly because most countries established bilateral trade agreements, thus precluding any sort of broad multilateral trade agreement).

[2] *See* STIGLITZ, *supra* Chapter I note 2, at 107 (explaining that these policies became known as "beggar–thy–neighbor" policies). Beggar–thy–neighbor policies are a government's protectionist course of action taken to discourage imports by raising tariffs and instituting nontariff barriers, usually to reduce domestic unemployment and increase domestic output. *Id.* This term is sometimes applied to competitive currency devaluation. *Id.*

[3] *See* STIGLITZ, *supra* Chapter I note 2, at 11–13 (asserting that contrary to its original policies, the IMF lends funds only if countries "engage in policies like cutting deficits, raising taxes, or raising interest rates that lead to a contraction of the economy.").

[4] *See* CHARLES P. KINDLEBERGER, THE WORLD IN DEPRESSION: 1929–1939, 26–8 (1973) (discussing how beggar–thy–neighbor tactics put countries in a worse–off position, since

1944 Bretton Woods Conference

In July 1944, delegates from forty-four allied nations[5] gathered at the Mount Washington Hotel in Bretton Woods, New Hampshire, with the objective of creating institutions that--through a unified system of purpose, policies, and rules--would regulate the international monetary system while simultaneously reconstructing the international relations

---

they led to retaliation among countries). National economic interests trumped international cooperation. *Id.* In addition to the British government's micromanagement of the agricultural industry, the 1932 Import Duties Act imposed an *ad valorem* tariff on almost all goods, with only minimal exceptions. *Id.* Further, the Ottawa Agreements Act granted a duty exemption for all British Commonwealth Countries; this led to the economic discrimination against Great Britain's neighboring countries. *Id.* at 85–86 (explaining further that the duty exemption granted reciprocity on duty–free imports and exports to all British Commonwealth Countries). Germany responded to the international financial crisis by establishing its own beggar–thy–neighbor policies in the form of exchange controls in 1931, and by 1933, several state import boards were granted the power to regulate trade through import quotas and tariffs. *Id. See* B. N. GHOSH, GLOBAL FINANCIAL CRISIS AND REFORMS: CASES AND CAVEATS 379 (2001) (explaining how Germany and France increased border protection and domestic market regulations). Parallel to the United Kingdom and Germany, most developed countries introduced exchange–control systems. DEREK HOWARD ALDCROFT, EUROPE'S THIRD WORLD: THE EUROPEAN PERIPHERY IN THE INTERWAR YEARS 61 (2006) (listing countries that established exchange controls during the 1930's as: Bulgaria 1931, Estonia 1931, Greece 1931, Hungary 1931, Latvia 1931, Lithuania 1935, Poland 1936, Romania 1932, Spain 1931, Turkey 1930, and Yugoslavia 1931). Those that did not introduce exchange systems became members of trade blocs similar to that of the British Commonwealth; these blocs were characterized by preferential trading agreements that benefited bloc members and discriminated against nonmembers. EUROPE IN THE INTERNATIONAL ECONOMY 1500 TO 2000 156 (Derek Howard Aldcroft & Anthony Sutcliffe eds., 1999) (explaining how exchange control systems were also an issue in the development of South American and African countries). Thirteen of the fourteen countries using these systems in the IMF were Latin American countries. *See id. See also* ELIZABETH HENNESSEY, A DOMESTIC HISTORY OF ENGLAND: 1930–1960, 85 (1992) (explaining how African countries fared differently under the exchange control systems depending upon their relationship with the British Commonwealth).

[5] *See* DEP'T OF STATE, *supra* Chapter I note 2. The forty–four nations were comprised of: Australia, Belgium, Bolivia, Brazil, Canada, Chile, China, Colombia, Costa Rica, Cuba, Czechoslovakia, Dominican Republic, Ecuador, Egypt, El Salvador, Ethiopia, France, Greece, Guatemala, Haiti, Honduras, Iceland, India, Iran, Iraq, Liberia, Luxembourg, Mexico, Netherlands, New Zealand, Nicaragua, Norway, Panama, Paraguay, Peru, Philippine Commonwealth, Poland, Union of South Africa, Union of Soviet Socialist Republics, United Kingdom, United States of America, Uruguay, Venezuela, and Yugoslavia. *Id.*

which had begun to develop before World War II.[6] Although all of the forty-four nations were present, the Bretton Woods agreement was largely negotiated between Britain and the United States of America.[7] The meeting resulted in the creation of the International Bank for Reconstruction and Development ("IBRD"), and the International Monetary Fund ("IMF").[8]

---

[6] DEP'T OF STATE, *supra* Ch. I note 2, at 5–7; *see also* DEP'T OF PUBLIC INFO, *supra* Ch. I note 2, at 365. The draft documents presented to delegates at the Bretton Woods conference were presented in four different versions: the U.S. version, the U.K. version, new material, and material taken from the Monetary Fund proposal. *See* MASON & ASHER, *supra* Ch. I note 3. Least developed members, including European countries damaged during World War II, held a greater interest in development of the IBRD than the IMF. *Id.* Therefore, when the first week of the conference primarily focused on development of the IMF, delegates feared the IBRD would not be established. *Id.* Stable monetary conditions are the cornerstone to successful lending and a precondition to the membership in the BWI. *Id.*; *see also* JACQUES J. POLAK, THE WORLD BANK AND THE IMF: A CHANGING RELATIONSHIP 1 (Brookings Inst., 1994). An attempt to reconcile openness and trade expansion with economic and employment stabilization, the agreement was "an unprecedented experiment in international economic constitution building." G. JOHN IKENBERRY, THE POLITICAL ORIGINS OF BRETTON WOODS, *in* A RETROSPECTIVE ON THE BRETTON WOODS SYSTEM 155 (1993).

[7] *See id.* The United States of America and Britain were the two major Western powers from World War II. *Id.*; *see also* ERIC HELLEINER, STATES AND THE REEMERGENCE OF GLOBAL FINANCE: FROM BRETTON WOODS TO THE 1990s 33 (1996) ("The Bretton Woods negotiations are often portrayed as a battle of wills between Keynes and White."); M.J. Stephey, *A Brief History of Bretton Woods System*, TIME (Oct. 21, 2008), http://content.time.com/time/business/article/0,8599,1852254,00.html (last visited Sept. 2, 2017).

[8] *See* PRESTON & WINDSOR, *supra* Ch. I note 2 (explaining that the names of these two institutions are somewhat confusing, since the IMF was established to carry out exchange, reserve, and short–term loan functions normally associated with "bank," while the IBRD is essentially a "Fund" for providing long–term loans). The IBRD was established on December 27, 1945 with the intent to:
"[A]ssist in the reconstruction and development of territories of members by facilitating the investment of capital for productive purposes; to promote private foreign investment and, when private investment is not readily available on reasonable terms, to supplement it by providing loans for productive purposes out of its own capital funds; and to promote the balanced growth of international trade and the maintenance of equilibrium in balances of payments by encouraging international investment for the development of the productive sources of the Bank's members." DEP'T OF PUBLIC INFO, *supra* Ch. I note 2, at 364–65. Membership to the IBRD is open to all members of the IMF. *Id.* at 364. The IMF was established with the purposes of facilitating international monetary cooperation; promoting exchange rate stability; assisting in the establishment of multilateral payment systems; eliminating foreign exchange restrictions; providing loans to nations

Despite the peaceful northern New Hampshire setting for the Bretton Woods conference, the meeting set the stage for future conflict not only between the United States and Great Britain, but also between historical differing economic policies. At the conference, Great Britain's Lord John Maynard Keynes ("Keynes") sought to retain the imperial preferential system and bilateral trading, while the United States' Harry Dexter White ("White") preferred an open, non-discriminatory multilateral trading system.[9]

The differing positions on how to create a global post-war economic foundation that emerged between the United States and Great Britain at the Bretton Woods conference stemmed from disagreement between British economist Keynes,[10] and American economist White,[11] the Unit-

---

experiencing balance of payments issues; all for the purpose of creating conditions for strong economic growth. *Id.* at 55.

[9] *See* IKENBERRY, *supra* note 6, at 156. Britain's position was to secure employment and economic stabilization within its borders for its citizens. *See id.* at 157. Formal negotiations on international trade took place in Havana, Cuba three years later under the formulation of the International Trade Organization. TYRONE FERGUSON, THIRD WORLD AND DECISION MAKING IN THE INTERNATIONAL MONETARY FUND 25 (Institut universitaire de hautes études internationales, 1988). The multilateral organization taking the place of the ITO was the General Agreement on Tariffs and Trade ("GATT") in 1947. *Id.* Analysts consider the Bretton Woods system's "triadic structure" to include the GATT, IMF, and IBRD, encompassing trade, monetary, and financial relations. *Id.* The GATT was intended to reverse protectionist and discriminatory trade practices such as the imperialistic approach. *See* General Agreement on Tariffs and Trade, Oct. 30, 1947, 61 Stat. A5, 55 U.N.T.S. 187, art. XV [hereinafter GATT].

[10] *See* Tejvan Pettinger, *John M. Keynes Biography*, BIOGRAPHY ONLINE (Feb 3, 2013), http://www.biographyonline.net/writers/keynes.html (last visited Sept. 2, 2017) (stating generally John Maynard Keynes was born in 1883 in an upper-middle class educated family); *see also* BENN STEIL, THE BATTLE OF BRETTON WOODS 61 (2013) (stating Keynes's father, John Neville Keynes, was a lecturer in moral sciences at the University of Cambridge and his mother, Florence Ada Keynes, graduated at Cambridge's Newman College then went to become the first woman mayor of Cambridge.); *Id.* at 62 (stating Keynes, a child prodigy, matriculated at Elton College at the age of fourteen (14), then he received a scholarship to attend Cambridge's Kings College); *Id.* (stating Keynes studied mathematics while in college and did not engage in the study of economic until after graduation under the guidance of Alfred Marshall); *Id.* (stating Keynes involvement in government began in 1906 when he served as a clerk in the Indian office for Her Majesty). *Id.* (stating Keynes vehemently argued for an increase in government spending to prevent economic recession). Keynes introduced his economic principles, which later

ed States Minister of State for the U.S. treasury.[12] Keynes[13] sought to retain the imperial preferential system and bilateral trading, while White[14] suggested an open, non-discriminatory multilateral trading system.[15] Despite their disagreement, White and Keynes agreed that

---

became known as Keynesian economics, during the Great Depression. *See* Sarwat Jahan et al., *What Is Keynesian Economics?*, INTERNATIONAL MONETARY FUND (Sep. 2014), http://www.imf.org/external/pubs/ft/fandd/2014/09/basics.htm (last visited Sept. 2, 2017) (stating Keynes' economic policy is based on three principal tenets, "(1) aggregate demand is influenced by many economic decisions—public and private; (2) prices, and especially wages, respond slowly to changes in supply and demand; and (3) changes in aggregate demand, whether anticipated or unanticipated, have their greatest short-run effect on real output and employment, not on prices."); *see also* Alan S. Blinder, *Keynesian Economics*, LIBRARY OF ECONOMICS AND LIBERTY, http://www.econlib.org/library/Enc/KeynesianEconomics.html. (last visited Sept. 2, 2017) Keynesian economics soared from the end of World War II until the 1970's when it became irresponsive to stagflation and critic from neo-classical economists and monetarists, such as Milton Friedman. *Id.* Nonetheless, Keynesian economic principles resurged during the recession in 2007-2008. *Id.*

[11] *See* STEIL, *supra* note 2, at 17–25 (stating Harry D. White was born in Boston in 1982 to immigrants from Lithuania.). White showed no particular early sign of brilliance, he began his collegiate career at the age of twenty-nine (29) after laboring at his father's hardware store and serving in the United States Army during World War I. *Id.* White earned his bachelor's and master's degree in economics at Stanford, and received his Ph.D. at Harvard. *Id.* Under the tutelage of Prof. Frank Taussing, White prepared his dissertation on the French International Accounts which won him the David A. Wells prize and was later published by Harvard University Press. *Id.* White had a brief career as a teacher prior to transitioning in governmental work. *Id.*

[12] *See, e.g.*, STIGLITZ, *supra* Chapter I note 2, at 173.

[13] *See* James M. Boughton, *Why White, not Keynes? Inventing the Postwar International Monetary System*, INTERNATIONAL MONETARY FUND (Mar. 2002), https://www.imf.org/external/pubs/ft/wp/2002/wp0252.pdf (last visited Sept. 2, 2017) (stating "Keynes was forced to fight a rearguard battle to prevent Britain from losing too much control over its finances.").

[14] *See* James Boughton, *Harry Dexter White and the History of Bretton Woods*, INSTITUTE FOR NEW ECONOMIC THINKING (Nov. 9, 2013), https://www.ineteconomics.org/perspectives/blog/harry-dexter-white-and-the-history-of-bretton-woods (last visited Sept. 2, 2017) (stating White's economic policy "favored a more rapid and complete opening up of trade and finance."); *see also* Boughton, *Why White, not Keynes? Inventing the Postwar International Monetary System*, *supra* note 13 (stating White favored a multilateral system over Keynes' bilateral financial assistance.).

[15] *See generally* G. John Ikenberry, Liberalism and Empire: Logics of Order in the American Unipolar Age 609-30 (2004) (stating the United States of America and Britain were the two major Western powers from World War II.); *See also* HELLEINER, *supra* note 7 (stating "[t]he Bretton Woods negotiations are often portrayed as a battle of wills between Keynes and White."); *see also* M.J. Stephey, *supra* note 7.

the rehabilitation of the world economy required the collaboration of every country rather than an autarkic economic system.[16] Keynes advocated for a system dominated by the two feuding states (i.e., Great Britain and the United States); however, White was successful in establishing a more multilateral institution.[17] Keynes's proposal, rooted in a theoretical International Clearing Union, promoted a system whereby the management and voting power of the financial institutions would be vested in the United States and Great Britain perpetually.[18] Although White was successful in using the United States' economic strength to establish an institution that preserved American interests, Keynes's true legacy was establishing global institutions that make it possible for other nations to stimulate aggregate demand, combined with a healthy dose of monetary policy, to maintain economic stability and fight crises as they arise.[19]

---

[16] *See* Boughton, *Why White, not Keynes? Inventing the Postwar International Monetary System*, *supra* note 13 (stating both "favored the active use of counter-cyclical policies to maintain high levels of employment . . . and favored adjustable exchange rates in support of open trade in goods and services, protected by a degree of control over capital flows."); *see also* James M. Boughton, *Harry Dexter White and the International Monetary Fund*, INTERNATIONAL MONETARY FUND (Sept. 1998), http://www.imf.org/external/pubs/ft/fandd/1998/09/boughton.htm (last visited Sept. 2, 2017) (stating Keynes and White agreed on "avoid[ing] the mistakes made after the First World War . . . [and] the international flow of capital should encourage trade and not be allowed to become an independent and possibly disruptive force."). *See* Boughton, *Harry Dexter White and the History of Bretton Woods*, *supra* note 14 (stating "[a] central element of what Keynes and White were trying to create was a way to have stable exchange rates and prices and economic growth.").

[17] *See* Boughton, *Why White, not Keynes? Inventing the Postwar International Monetary System*, *supra* note 13 (stating "Keynes'[] resistance to multilateralism was grounded in the need to preserve Britain's special status through its central role in the Empire and its bilateral relationship with the United States.")

[18] *Id.*

[19] *See* Sarwat Jahan, et al., *supra* note 10 (providing a brief account of the development and significance of Keynesian Economics); *see also* N. Gregory Mankiw, What Would Keynes Have Done? NEW YORK TIMES (Nov. 28, 2008) http://www.nytimes.com/2008/11/30/business/economy/30view.html (last visited Sept. 2, 2017) (arguing that Keynesian Economic theory continue to be an effective mechanism to combat economic crises similar to the Great Recession of the last decade). Keynesian economics entails a short-term stimulation of aggregate demand combined with long term monetary policy. *Id.* The BWI provide an alternative source of financing for mem-

Fundamentally, Great Britain recognized a need for some post–war regulation on the international scene; it recognized that the potential exploitation by the war's victors of the defeated Axis Powers--as a means of financing the reconstruction of war-torn European nations-- could lead to another global disaster.[20] The United States' influence and power ultimately won out, for the BWI were mostly modeled after White's proposals.[21]

After Bretton Woods Conference

Throughout the 1960s, the BWI faced three significant obstacles: decolonization, threats of decreasing international liquidity, and a weakening gold standard.[22] In partial response, the World Bank created the

---

ber states to stimulate aggregate demand, especially when some members would find it difficult to finance or secure these loans independently. *Id.*

[20] *See* JOHN D. CIORCIARI, *The Lawful Scope of Human Rights Criteria in World Bank Credit Decisions: An Interpretive Analysis of the IBRD and IDA Articles of Agreement*, 33 CORNELL INT'L L. J 361-69 (2000) (describing the negotiations leading up to the creation of the BWI that took place prior to the end of WWII; *World War II*, U.S. HISTORY, http://www.u-s-history.com/pages/h1661.html (last visited Sept. 2, 2017) (explaining that the Allies were determined not to repeat the mistakes of World War I); Paul Wachtel, *Understanding the Old and New Bretton Woods* 6 NEW YORK UNIVERSITY, STERN SCHOOL OF BUSINESS (Jan. 4, 2007), http://w4.stern.nyu.edu/emplibrary/Florence_paper_jan4.pdf (last visited Sept. 2, 2017). Keynes proposed an international bank and a radical institutional system for management of currencies, including creation of a common world–unit of currency. *Id.* He envisioned that these institutions would manage international trade through regulation and prove strong incentives for countries to avoid substantial trade deficits while fostering economic growth. *Id.* Meanwhile, White's proposal called for less regulation. *Id.* White proposed limited government interference and gave more emphasis to market based solutions. *Id.*

[21] *See* Sabine Dammasch, *The System of Bretton Woods: A Lesson from History*, THE HIDDEN MYSTERY SERIES (June 6, 2017) http://www.ww.uni-magdeburg.de/fwwdeka/student/arbeiten/006.pdf (last visited Sept. 2, 2017).

[22] *See* JONG IL YOU, THE BRETTON WOODS INSTITUTIONS: EVOLUTION, REFORM AND CHANGE, IN GOVERNING GLOBALIZATION: ISSUES AND INSTITUTIONS, IN DEEPAK NAYYAR, GOVERNING GLOBALIZATION: ISSUES AND INSTITUTIONS 209-12 (2000) (explaining that SDR's were created in 1969 to respond to the shortage of international liquidity); *Historical Gold Prices – 1833 to Present*, NATIONAL MINING ASSOCIATION, http://nma.org/wp-content/uploads/2016/08/Historical-Gold-Prices.pdf (last visited Sept. 2, 2017) (listing the price of gold from 1833 to present day).

International Development Association ("IDA")[23] in 1960, which was praised as "the most significant moment in institutional expansion of the BWI toward a poverty–focused approach." [24]   When Robert McNamara arrived as World Bank President in 1968, the Bank's fundraising efforts grew.[25] Envisioning a larger, more active, and more efficient bank, McNamara established lending targets which, due to acceleration of the Bank's growth, justified reorganization in 1973.[26]

The IDA,[27] led by the United States, assisted the world's most impoverished countries, which were ineligible for bank loans, by offering con-

---

[23] *See* International Development Association, *Articles of Agreement and Report of the Executive Directors of the International Bank for Reconstruction and Development on the Articles of Agreement*, (Sept. 24, 1960), at 21 [hereinafter "IDA Articles of Agreement"].

[24] *See* Balakrishnan Rajagopal, *From Resistance to Renewal: Third World Social Movements and International Institutions*, 41 HARV. INT'L L.J. 529, 552 (2000) (explaining how the IDA led to the further establishment of additional development institutions because its framework, lending primarily to Third World countries, helped the World Bank become a true international institution).

[25] *Id.* at 140, 180; *see* Jochen Kraske, et al., Bankers with a Mission: The Presidents of the World Bank, 1946–1991 at 175 (Oxford University Press, 1996); PHILIPPE LE PRESTRE, The World Bank and the Environmental Challenge 59 (Susquehanna University Press, 1989). McNamara's stated reorganization goal was to:
"[r]eplace the . . . procedure in which unrelated project loans, considered in isolation from another, filter up through the levels with a five-year program based on systems analysis and overall development strategy, taking account of relative priorities among countries and within sectors of each country, as directed from the top."
Id.; see also Enrique R. Carrasco & M. Ayhan Kose, *Symposium: Social Justice and Development: Critical Issues Facing the Bretton Woods System: Income Distribution and the Bretton Woods Institutions: Promoting an Enabling Environment for Social Development*, 6 TRANSNAT'L L. & CONTEMP. PROBS. 1, 18 (1996). Lending to alleviate poverty in developing countries expanded considerably after Robert McNamara took over the Bank's helm in the late 1960's; structural adjustment lending followed in the late 1970's. *Id.; see also* KRASKE, *supra* note 25, at 140 (discussing how during McNamara's presidency, the World Bank staff tripled, growing from 1,600 to 5,700 people).

[26] *See* SEBASTIAN MALLABY, THE WORLD'S BANKER 26–27 (2004) (discussing the divergence of the World Bank from a conservative lender to an ambitious bank set on offering loans to countries even if they could not afford to pay them back). The creation of the IDA reflected a shifting mind–set of the World Bank's largest shareholders as they saw the tide of independence sweeping Africa, combined with the height of the Cold War, as an opportunity to aid others in the hopes that those governments aided through the IDA would not become communist. *Id.*

[27] *See* IDA Articles of Agreement, *supra* note 23 (discussing how the United States and a group of the Bank's member countries set up an agency that would lend to the poorest countries with the most favorable terms possible).

cessional or soft loans.[28] Shifting its attention to newly industrializing countries in Africa, Asia, and Latin America, the World Bank expanded its reach into new sectors.[29] The IDA's funding was derived from the contributions of wealthier nations, IBRD income, and borrowers' credit repayments.[30] Due to the fact that funds were initially insufficient to meet the IDA's commitments--because of the unlikelihood of substantial replenishment due to the balance of payment deficit experienced by wealthier states--there emerged a certain skepticism about progress, which contributed to delays associated with recuperating the funds.[31]

---

[28] *See* DEVESH KAPUR, JOHN P. LEWIS & BERNARD WEBB, THE WORLD BANK: ITS FIRST HALF CENTURY VOL. 2 PERSPECTIVES 204, 207 (1997) (explaining how the United States encouraged the World Bank during the establishment of IDA to extend lending to low–income countries, become involved in development problems such as agricultural productivity, and take the lead in matters relating to industrial and trade liberation in India); *see e.g.,* OECD, *Concessional Loans,* http://stats.oecd.org/glossary/detail.asp?ID=5901 (last visited Sept. 2, 2017) (defining concessional loans as "loans that are extended on terms substantially more generous than market loans; the concessionality is achieved either through interest rates below those available on the market or by grace periods, or a combination of these. Concessional loans typically have long grace periods.").

[29] *See* Martin A. Weiss, *CRS Report for Congress: The World Bank's International Development Association (IDA)* 2, 6 (Apr. 1, 2008), https://www.google.com/url?sa=t&rct=j&q=&esrc=s&source=web&cd=1&ved=0ahUKEwi otoD5qZrTAhWJ7iYKHZBRB2UQFggfMAA&url=http%3A%2F%2Fresearch.policyarchiv e.org%2F3225.pdf&usg=AFQjCNGNPLLaGAMC1VbrvZW5RNM1XunRxg&sig2=VOKlS wW2HcBc-7EKy3u6RQ (explaining how concerns of the World Bank loans being unaffordable to low–income countries prompted the establishment of the IDA); *see also* International Development Association, *supra* note 23; *What is IDA?,* THE WORLD BANK, http://ida.worldbank.org/about/what-ida (last visited Sept. 2, 2017). The IDA–15 replenishment raised funds for poor countries for the three–year period between July 2008 and June 2011. *Id.* These are critical years for countries trying to achieve the U.N. Millennium Development Goals since it takes time for projects to be completed and yield measurable results. *Id.* Forty–five donor countries made pledges toward this replenishment. *Id.*

[30] *See generally* KRASKE, *supra* note 25, at 142–43 (explaining that IDA commitments dropped in 1968 from $400 million per year to $107 million). This became a problem of mobilizing resources within the IDA. *Id.*

[31] *Id.* This became a problem of mobilizing resources within the IDA. *Id.* at 140, 180; EDITH KUIPER & DRUCILLA K. BARKER, FEMINIST ECONOMICS AND THE WORLD BANK: HISTORY, THEORY AND POLICY 17 (Routledge, 2006) ("A critical junction in the Bank's history was the appointment as its president of Robert McNamara. . . . During his tenure . . . the Bank shifted from an emphasis on infrastructure to agriculture and rural development, in an attempt to address people's basic needs, particularly the rural poor.").

As time passed, however, a significant and problematic shift emerged in the IDA's operational philosophy. It moved away from the World Bank's original theory of market-based lending, and instead adopted a new theory favoring loans to the poorest countries.[32] These loans were then furnished at cheaper rates, under the guise of giving "World Bank credits as a useful tool for propping up sympathetic governments."

Originally, the cornerstone of the Bretton Woods system had been the United States' policy of buying and selling gold according to an official price set at the behest of foreign monetary authorities.[33] The Bretton Woods Articles of Agreement, Article IV, defined the unit of the international monetary system as either the U.S. dollar or gold of a specified weight and fineness.[34] However, the vulnerability of the gold standard

---

[32] *See* Carrasco & Kose, *supra* note 25, at 3.
Income inequality came under scrutiny during preparatory meetings for the World Summit for Social Development (Social Summit). Observers noted that although living standards in developing countries have improved over the past two decades, disparities within countries–the subject of this article–are likely to rise, with the largest gaps occurring in South Asia, Latin America, and the Caribbean.
Id.; see also DIGUMARTI BHASKARA RAO, WORLD SUMMIT FOR SOCIAL DEVELOPMENT 198 (1998) (quoting former secretary general Boutros–Ghali); *See* LE PRESTRE, *supra* note 25, for a discussion on the BWI involvement in the development debate of the 1960's and 1970's. *See id.*

[33] MICHAEL D. BORDO & BARRY EICHENGREEN, *Bretton Woods and the Great Inflation* 28 (Soc. Sci. Res. Network, Working Paper No. w14532, 2008) (explaining how first, there was an asymmetric adjustment between deficit and surplus countries, which led to a deflationary bias); *see* FRITZ MACHLUP, REMAKING THE INTERNATIONAL MONETARY SYSTEM: THE RIO AGREEMENT AND BEYOND 7–8 (Committee for Economic, 1968) (explaining how the United Kingdom and United States conflicted over the gold standard because the United States and White wanted it, but the United Kingdom and Keynes saw the system as imposing intolerable restraints on member countries). Gold supplies were inadequate to finance the growth of world output, and to serve as gold cover to back national currencies. BORDO & EICHENGREEN, *supra*. Shifts of currency holdings between London and New York risked a confidence crisis in the weak sector, while a shift between the key currencies and gold occurred when foreign holders of key currency balances staged runs on banks where reserve centers' could not convert their outstanding liabilities into gold. *Id.*

[34] BAHRAM GHAZI, THE IMF, THE WORLD BANK GROUP AND THE QUESTION OF HUMAN RIGHTS 3 (Transnational Publishers, 2005) (explaining how other IMF members also had to keep the value of their currency within one percent of the par value). If a change of margin was needed, IMF members had to undergo thorough discussions with other members and obtain their consent before implementing the measure. *Id.*

began to show in the 1960s. Later, in August 1971, President Richard Nixon officially suspended the automatic conversion of dollars into other currencies.[35] Although solutions to fixing the gold standard for the international monetary system were proposed, ultimately the Bretton Woods gold-standard system collapsed. This led to the development of Special Drawing Rights ("SDR")[36] in 1969.[37] Essentially, SDR are "[i]nternational reserve asset(s) [which] supplement existing reserve assets."[38]

"While pressure for good governance has been magnified by the policy role of the Bretton Woods twins [also known as the IMF and World Bank], neither institution has adequately reformed [the] core aspects of

---

[35] *See id; see also* THE ECONOMIST, *A Brief History of Funny Money*, Jan. 6, 1990, at 21 (providing a brief account of why the Bretton Woods system ended and a larger debate as to which exchange–rate system has worked best in the world economy).

[36] *See Special Drawing Rights (SDR)*, INTERNATIONAL MONETARY FUND, http://www.imf.org/external/np/exr/facts/sdr.HTM (last visited Sept. 2, 2017) [hereinafter "SDR"] (discussing the makeup of the SDR). The SDR is a potential claim on the freely usable currencies of IMF members where holders of SDR can obtain currencies in exchange for their SDR through the arrangement of voluntary exchanges between IMF members, or through an IMF designation of members with strong external positions to purchase SDR from members with weak external positions. *Id.; Held in Reserve: A Brief Guide to the IMF's "Currency"*, THE ECONOMIST (Apr. 8, 2009), http://www.economist.com/node/13447239 (discussing the redefinition of the SDR as a basket of currencies consisting of the value of a fixed amount of the Japanese yen, U.S. dollar, pound sterling, and Euro).

[37] *Id.* (discussing how various sources of liquidity became unreliable and inadequate toward financing the growth of output and trade). In the late 1950's the world's monetary gold stock became insufficient. *Id.* The supply of U.S. dollars was dependent on the U.S. balance of payments, which hedged on the "vagaries of government policy and the confidence problem." *Id.* The probability of all dollar holders being able to convert their dollars into gold at the fixed price declined" and "outstanding dollar liabilities held by the rest of the world monetary authorities increased relative to the U.S. monetary gold stock." *Id.; see also* Joseph Gold, *The "Sanctions" of the International Monetary Fund*, 66 AM. J. OF INT'L L. 737 (1972) (discussing the special drawing rights amendment to the IMF Articles, with a focus on sanctions); William Bernhard, J. Lawrence Broz & William Roberts Clark, *The Political Economy of Monetary Institutions*, 56 INT'L ORG. 693, 700 (2002) (discussing the gold overhand and lax U.S. macroeconomic policies).

[38] *See* Editorial, *The G–20's Funny Money*, WALL ST. J., Apr. 1, 2009, at A22 (originally, to participate in this system, a country needed official reserves, government or central bank holdings of gold, and widely accepted foreign currencies that could be used to purchase the domestic currency in foreign exchange markets. After the Bretton Woods system collapsed, the major currencies shifted to a floating exchange-rate).

accountability and participation."[39] SDR have been criticized as funny money, as nothing more than a fancy term for allocated credits that have no value and which the IMF doles out to member countries, but that can be exchanged for subsidized loans to non-reserve currency countries.[40] Because SDR are allocated in proportion to countries' existing IMF quotas, when the G20[41] countries authorized the IMF to issue $250 billion in new SDR in 2009, up to approximately $170 billion could still land in the reserves of wealthy countries such as the United States, Japan, and Britain.[42] Although the IMF hopes the reserve-rich countries will lend their shares to those countries in greater need, this is not a guarantee required by the current system.[43]

_____

[39] *See* Ngaire Woods, *Governance in International Organizations: The Case for Reform in the Bretton Woods Institutions*, INT'L AND FIN. MONETARY ISSUES (2008), http://www.globaleconomicgovernance.org/wp-content/uploads/Governance%20and%20Decision-Making.pdf (last visited Dec. 3, 2013).
[40] *Held in Reserve, supra* note 36 (discussing the April 2, 2009 authorization of $250 billion in fresh SDR). Another example is China; its SDR reserves, already nearly $2 trillion, will go up $9.3 billion. *Id.; see* SDR, *supra* note 36 (discussing how the IMF allocates SDR). Under the Articles of Agreement, the IMF may allocate SDR to members in proportion to their respective IMF quotas using two kinds of allocations: general and special. *Id.* General allocations are based on a long–term global need to supplement existing reserve assets, and have only been made three times, where special allocations occur in the form of a one–time allocation of SDR enabling all members of the IMF to participate in the SDR system on an equitable basis. *Id.* This corrects the inequity for countries that joined the IMF after 1981, as they had never received an SDR allocation. *Id.* The three general allocations were distributed in 1970 through 1972, 1979 through 1981, and on August 28, 2009; the special allocation was implemented on September 9, 2009. *Id.*
[41] *See Held in Reserve, supra* note 36 (explaining that the United States needs Congressional approval to part with its share). The last proposed SDR allocation in 1997 failed because only 75% of the votes accepted the proposal, and the IMF requirement is 85% of votes in order for the allocation to be ratified. *Id.* The United States, with nearly seventeen percent of the votes in the IMF, never approved. *Id.; see also The G–20's Funny Money, supra* note 38 (explaining how SDR cost U.S. taxpayers $330 million per year). Had the 1997 resolution been approved, U.S. exposure would have been about $12 billion with a $750 million annual cost to taxpayers. *The G–20's Funny Money, supra* note 38. Although IMF financing does not show up on the annual United States expenditure, the SDR credits make countries in turmoil, such as Syria, Zimbabwe, Sudan, Venezuela, and Burma, eligible for substantial amounts of money. *Id.*
[42] *See Held in Reserve, supra* note 36; *see also The G–20's Funny Money, supra* note 38.
[43] *See Voting Powers*, THE WORLD BANK (Jan. 10, 2010),

Voting Structures

International Monetary Fund

The IMF's voting structure was at the outset a topic of debate among the principal founding nations.[44] Despite the desire of many countries to institute purely economic criteria in determining how votes would be distributed, the votes were allocated based on the relative economic importance of member-states to the international economy.[45] In order to appease smaller economic nations, the weighted voting system was bifurcated to include the allocation of a certain number of "basic" votes, which would be guaranteed to each member, thus giving smaller countries a "sense of participation," and tempering the overriding control that would be exercised by larger countries.[46] Also, while majority-voting for decision-making was to be a requisite in the IMF's Articles, the United States successfully advocated that certain decisions should require higher majorities for approval.[47] Despite the attempt to evenly

---

http://www.worldbank.org/en/about/leadership/votingpowers [hereinafter "Voting Powers"] (providing links to voting statuses of the IBRD, IFC, IDA, and MIGA listed by country and executive director).

[44] *See* J. KEITH HORSEFIELD, THE INTERNATIONAL MONETARY FUND 1945–1965: TWENTY YEARS OF INTERNATIONAL MONETARY COOPERATION 59 (International Monetary Fund, 1969) ("It would be an advantage if the proposed Union could be brought into existence by the United States and the United Kingdom as joint founder–States . . . [t]he management and the effective voting powers might adhere permanently in the founder States."). *See* Michael Tanzer, *Globalizing the Economy: the Influence of the International Monetary Fund and the World Bank*, MONTHLY REV., Sept. 1, 1995 at 1 (discussing how the United States was ensured to be the dominant voice, having thirty–six percent of the subscribed capital).

[45] *See* FERGUSON, *supra* note 9, at 60–61.

[46] *See* Tanzer, *supra* note 44; *see also* FERGUSON, *supra* note 9, at 60–61 (explaining that although this requirement effectively gave the United States a unilateral veto power, it was added to the Fund's Articles albeit in a more limited version in which the high, special majorities would be reserved for a few important decisions).

[47] *See* Articles of Agreement of International Monetary Fund. Art. V, s. 5–7, http://www.imf.org/external/pubs/ft/aa/pdf/aa.pdf (last visited Sept. 2, 2017). Repurchase of currency and dealings of special drawing rights are some examples of instances which require super majority approval. *See id.* The voting structure provides that, when a vote is needed to waive any conditions on loan eligibility or even to declare a member country ineligible for IMF funds, the member's votes shall be increased by each 400,000 special

allocate a certain percentage of votes to smaller countries, subsequent IMF practice--and the increase in the number of smaller economies as members of the IMF--led to a reduction in the proportionality of basic votes as compared with total voting power.[48]

To fully analyze the voting requirements and their effects on the many nations, an analysis of the IMF's overall governance structure and implementation is required.[49] The IMF is governed by a Board of Governors that meets once each year and consists of one governor and one alternate governor for each member country.[50] The day-to-day business of the IMF is handled by a twenty-four member Executive Board of Directors.[51] In some cases, such as in Africa, just one director represents dozens of countries, each with their own unique linguistic and cultural tradition.[52]

---

drawing rights of net sales and reduced for each 400,000 special drawing rights of net purchases. *Id.* at Art. XII, s. 5.

[48] *See* Hector Torres, *Reforming the International Monetary Fund–Why its Legitimacy is at Stake*, 10 J. INT'L ECON. L. 443, 446 (2007) (explaining Torres' experience within the Fund and that the imbalance in voting power leads to the dilution of a true consensus voting forum, thereby falsifying by effect the Fund's frequent statements that its decisions are mostly taken by consensus); *see e.g.*, *IMF Members' Quotas and Voting Power, and IMF Board of Governors*, INT'L MONETARY FUND (July 11, 2011), http://www.imf.org/external/np/sec/memdir/members.aspx (last visited Sept. 2, 2017). *See* FERGUSON, *supra* note 9 (emphasizing that votes are distributed according to quotas and quotas are meant to reflect wealth. G7 countries alone have 41.72% of votes and 28 countries hold over 61% of the voting power at both the Fund and the World Bank).

[49] *See* Alexander Mountford, *Independent Evaluation Office Background Paper of the International Monetary Fund, The Formal Governance Structure of the Monetary Fund* (March 2001), http://www.imf.org/external/about/govstruct.htm (last visited Sept. 2, 2017).

[50] *Id.; see Factsheet: A Guide To Committees, Groups, and Clubs*, INT'L MONETARY FUND, http://www.imf.org/external/np/exr/facts/groups.htm#IC (last visited Sept. 2, 2017) [hereinafter "IMF Factsheet"] (providing a general discussion of the IMFC and explaining that larger economies, mirroring the weighted-voting philosophy, are represented by individual directors while smaller economies—developing countries—are grouped together and represented by a single director). During meetings, the governors vote on various amendments to the structure and operation of the IMF. *Id.* Each governor, usually the minister of finance or the head of the central bank within his or her country, is appointed by his or her respective member country. *Id.*

[51] *See IMF Executive Directors and Voting Power*, INT'L MONETARY FUND, https://www.imf.org/external/np/sec/memdir/eds.aspx (last visited Sept. 2, 2017).

[52] *See IMF Factsheet, supra* note 51.

The IMF has two ministerial committees: the International Monetary and Financial Committee ("IMFC"),[53] and the Development Committee (jointly with the Bank).[54] The ministerial composition of these two committees is basically identical to the composition of the respective Executive Boards.

World Bank

The planning process to create the World Bank was significantly less rigorous than the planning required for the creation of the IMF.[55] White's initial plan for a postwar stabilization fund and international bank included voting in proportion to stock holding.[56] However, his ultimate plan proposed voting power by the number of shares held by each government.[57] Ultimately, subscriptions to the capital of the Bank determined voting power, and thus, the World Bank's use of the weighted voting system is almost identical to the IMF's.[58] Despite a

---

[53] *See id.* (discussing the Development Committee); *see also* William N. Gianaris, *Weighted Voting in the International Monetary Fund and the World Bank*, 14 FORDHAM INT'L L.J. 910, 914 (1990) (The IMFC discusses matters of concern affecting the global economy).

[54] *See IMF Executive Directors and Voting Power*, INT'L MONETARY FUND, http://www.imf.org/external/np/sec/memdir/eds.htm (last updated Oct. 2, 2017). The Development Committee advises the Boards of Governors of the IMF and the World Bank on issues related to economic development in emerging and developing countries. *Governance Structure*, INT'L MONETARY FUND (last visited Sept. 2, 2017), http://www.imf.org/external/about/govstruct.htm; The Boards of Governors appoints or elects the Executive Board. *IMF Executive Directors and Voting Powers, supra.* The Executive Board takes care of the daily business of the IMF. *Id.*

[55] *See* MASON & ASHER, *supra* Chapter I note 1, at 14–16 (explaining how the Inter–American Bank combined the functions of an ordinary commercial bank, intergovernmental bank, and international stabilization fund).

[56] *See id.* (explaining that no government could hold more than twenty–five percent of the total voting power).

[57] *See id.*

[58] *See* Gianaris, *supra* note 53, at 917–18, 927–28 (discussing further that although membership in the World Bank is contingent upon membership in the IMF, the reverse is not true).
Like the IMF, each member has 250 basic votes plus one additional vote for each share of capital equivalent to U.S. $100,000 subscribed . . . While most states wanted a large quota in the IMF, giving them enhanced drawing rights, the less developed countries preferred a lower quota in the World Bank because the amount they could borrow was independ-

revision of the voting structure in 2010, the six largest economies of the 187 member countries still maintain 38.61% of the total vote, with the United States having 15.85% alone.[59]

Similar to the governing structure of the IMF, the World Bank's powers are vested in its Board of Governors.[60] Another analogous feature is that the Board of Executive Directors for the World Bank has all of the day-to-day powers. The Articles of Agreement set forth the structure and powers of the Board of Governors and the Board of Executive Directors. Of the twenty-four Executive Directors, the five largest shareholders are France, Germany, Japan, the United Kingdom, and the United States.[61] Interestingly enough, each of the eleven Presidents of the World Bank, also known as the Chairman of the Board of Executive Directors, have been the appointed Executive Director of the United States.[62]

Critique of Voting Structures

Both IMF member countries and critics of the IMF have attacked the IMF's voting structure, characterizing it as outdated.[63] In response to

---

ent of their capital contribution. To resolve the controversy, the United States agreed to accept a larger quota in the World Bank than in the IMF.
Id.

[59] *See Members,* INT'L MONETARY FUND,
http://www.imf.org/external/np/sec/memdir/members.aspx (last visited Sept. 2, 2017). The United States currently has 16.75% of the voting power. *Id.*

[60] *See Board of Governors, IMF, Articles of Agreement, art. XII, Section 2* THE WORLD BANK, http://go.worldbank.org/L46NF9XJ40 (last visited Sept. 3, 2017) (stating the World Bank's Board of Governors consist of one governor and one alternate governor appointed by each member country).

[61] *See About the World Bank,* THE WORLD BANK,
http://www.worldbank.org/en/about/leadership/directors (last visited Sept. 3, 2017). (Each appoints an individual Executive Director while the remaining nineteen Executive Directors represent the other 182 member countries).

[62] *Id.*

[63] *See* Jonathan Gregson, *The World Bank: Trying Times,* GLOBAL FIN., Oct. 2007, at 24 (discussing how emerging countries want a greater say within the World Bank's voting structure). India and Brazil are examples of emerging economies which have criticized the IMF's voting structures as being outdated and who believe that as a result of their respective increased contributing to the global economy, they should henceforth be provided with voting powers which correlate. *Id.* ARIEL BUIRA, CHALLENGES TO THE WORLD

such criticisms, the IMF issued proposals to change the voting structure, such as a one-time boost in voting power to under-represented countries and an increase in the developing nations' voting share coupled with a respective decrease in the voting share of some of the industrial nations, especially those in Europe.[64] Yet, these proposed changes were not without their own set of criticisms.[65]

BANK AND IMF: DEVELOPING COUNTRY PERSPECTIVES 1 (2003); *see also* JOHN E. CHEN, THE ROLE OF INTERNATIONAL INSTITUTIONS IN GLOBALIZATION: THE CHALLENGES OF REFORM 81 (2003); M. PANIC, GLOBALIZATION AND NATIONAL ECONOMIC WELFARE 228 (2003); WILLIAM K. TABB, ECONOMIC GOVERNANCE IN THE AGE OF GLOBALIZATION 184, 373 (2004); V. SPIKE PETERSON, A CRITICAL REWRITING OF GLOBAL POLITICAL ECONOMY: INTEGRATED, REPRODUCTIVE AND VIRTUAL ECONOMIES 3, 8 (2003); JEFFREY D. SACHS, THE ANTI–GLOBALIZATION MOVEMENT, THE GLOBALIZATION AND DEVELOPMENT READER: PERSPECTIVE ON DEVELOPMENT AND SOCIAL CHANGE 356 (2007); JOSEPH STIGLITZ, GLOBALISM'S DISCONTENTS, THE GLOBALIZATION AND DEVELOPMENT READER: PERSPECTIVE ON DEVELOPMENT AND SOCIAL CHANGE 295 (2007); Messner et al., *Governance Reform of the Bretton Woods Institutions and the U.N. Development System* 6 (Friedrich Ebert Stiftung: Dialogue on Globalization, Occasion Paper No. 18, 2005). The IMF and the World Bank have a weighted system of voting. *Articles of Agreement of the International Monetary Fund*, INTERNATIONAL MONETARY FUND, http://www.imf.org/external/pubs/ft/aa/aa12.htm#5 (last visited Sept. 3, 2017) [hereinafter "Articles of IMF"] (explaining subsection a); *see* WORLD BANK, *Voting Powers*, http://www.worldbank.org/en/about/leadership/votingpowers (last visited Sept. 3, 2017) [hereinafter "Voting Powers"] (explaining that the IMF's voting bylaws state that each member is guaranteed 250 votes, plus one additional vote for each part of its quota equal to 100,000 special drawing rights. Within the World Bank, a new member country is allotted 250 votes plus one additional vote for each share it holds in the World Bank's capital stock); *see also ICSID Basic Documents*, ICSID (last visited Sept. 3, 2017), https://icsid.worldbank.org/en/Pages/icsiddocs/Overview.aspx (discussing how the ICSID allocates its voting within its Administrative Council; all decisions are taken by a majority of the votes cast, and each member must vote in person).

[64] *See* Anthony Faiola, *Nations Cast Plan for Expanded IMF: Role to Deepen in Global Economy*, WASH. POST, Oct. 7, 2009, at A18 (explaining the preliminary plan that, by January 2011, would give more voting power to emerging financial powers like Brazil and China). Emerging economies would have more long–term say over the IMF's policies if voting rights were redistributed, "giving a 50–50 split to the developing and developed worlds." *Id.; see also* IMF Board of Governors Approves Quota and Related Governance Reforms (Sept. 18, 2006), http://www.imf.org/external/np/sec/pr/2006/pr06205.htm (last visited Sept. 3, 2017) (explaining how on September 18, 2006, the IMF's Board of Governors adopted a resolution that aimed to align the IMF's quota shares with members' positions within the world economy). Mexico, China, Korea, and Turkey, which were characterized as underrepresented countries, gained an increase in quota shares. *Id. But see Intergovernmental Group of Twenty–Four on International Monetary Affairs and Development Communiqué* (Oct. 10, 2008), http://www.imf.org/external/np/cm/2008/101008.htm

The "basic vote" of the IMF was originally a compromise to give developing countries a specified number of votes on top of the allocated "quota-based" votes.[66] Since 1944, the IMF's quota has increased by a factor of thirty-seven while its membership has quadrupled.[67] Originally, basic votes accounted for 11.3 percent of all votes but that has been reduced to merely 2.1 percent. This drastic decline in the power of the basic vote "has substantially shifted the balance of power in favor of large-quota countries .... Consequently, the voice of small countries in discussions has been substantially weakened and their participation in decision–making made negligible."[68] The result of the weighted voting structure is that developed countries have 60.4 percent of the IMF's voting power, while only accounting for twenty percent of the IMF's membership and fifteen percent of the world's population.[69]

Realizing a need for some sort of voting reform, the IMF is in the process of instituting amendments to the overall voting structure after the

---

(explaining that an agreement was not reached on an increase in the voting power of developing and transition countries). It was stressed that broader objectives were necessary to achieve a realignment of voting shares because the current proposal at the time was a piece–meal approach. *Id.*

[65] *See* Christopher Swann, *Critics Assail IMF Plan on Developing Nations' Voting Share,* WASH. POST, Mar. 29, 2008, at D03 (discussing a 2008 plan that intended to give more voting authority to developing countries). The voting share of developing countries was to rise to forty–two percent from about 40.5% while the voting share of advanced economies would have fallen from 59.5% to 58%. *Id.* Former IMF officials, such as former chief economist at the U.S. agency for International Development Colin Bradford and former executive vice president with the Inter–American Development Bank Nancy Birdsall signed a letter authored by former assistant Treasury secretary Edwin M. Truman expressing their displeasure with the proposed reforms because they fell short in "addressing the challenges facing the IMF and its evolution toward a truly global institution. *Id.*

[66] *See* JAMES M. BOUGHTON & DOMENICO LOMBARDI, FINANCE, DEVELOPMENT, AND THE IMF 290 (2009) (stating that the compromise was to allocate 250 "basic votes" to each member country).

[67] *See* DAVID WOODWARD, UNITED NATIONS CONFERENCE ON TRADE AND DEVELOPMENT, G-24 DISCUSSION PAPER SERIES, IMF VOTING REFORM: NEED, OPPORTUNITY AND OPTIONS 1 (United Nations Publication, 2007).

[68] *See* BUIRA, *supra* note 63, at 15.

[69] *See* WOODWARD, *supra* note 67, at 2.

Board of Governors approved such reform on December 15, 2010.[70] In 2008, reforms passed increasing basic votes to 5.502 percent of total votes, which results in 741 basic votes for each of the 187 member countries of the IMF.[71] Additionally, the reform enabled Executive Directors representing seven or more members to each appoint second Alternate Executive Director following the 2012 regular elections of Executive Director.[72] Unfortunately, despite the much needed reform, developed countries still maintain a large percentage of the IMF's voting power; the seven G7 countries alone maintain 43.12 percent of all the votes while the top ten quota-based countries, including the G7 countries, have 52.13 percent of all the votes.[73]

---

[70] *See IMF Quota and Governance Publications*, IMF (last visited Sept. 3, 2017), http://www.imf.org/external/np/fin/quotas/pubs/index.htm. Even more drastic than the 2008 reforms, the Board of Governors, on December 15, 2010, passed a package of far-reaching reforms, completing the "14th General Review of Quotas." *Id.* The 14th General Review of Quotas will: 1) double quotas from approximately SDR 238.4 billion to approximately SDR 476.8 billion, (about US$767 billion at current exchange rates); 2) shift more than 6 percent of quota shares from over-represented to under-represented member countries; 3) shift more than 6 percent of quota shares to dynamic emerging market and developing countries (EMDCs); 4) significantly realign quota shares. China will become the 3rd largest member country in the IMF, and there will be four EMDCs (Brazil, China, India, and Russia) among the 10 largest shareholders in the Fund; and 5) preserve the quota and voting share of the poorest member countries. This group of countries is defined as those eligible for the low-income Poverty Reduction and Growth Trust (PRGT) and whose per capita income fell below US$1,135 in 2008 (the threshold set by the International Development Association) or twice that amount for small countries. *Id.*

[71] *See Factsheet: IMF Quotas*, IMF (Sept. 13, 2011), http://www.imf.org/external/np/exr/facts/quotas.htm (last visited Sept. 3, 2017).

[72] *See* Press Release, Int'l Monetary Fund, IMF Executive Board Recommends Reforms to Overhaul Quota and Voice (Mar. 28, 2008), http://www.imf.org/external/np/sec/pr/2008/pr0864.htm (last visited Sept. 3, 2017) (stating that the Executive Directors of African countries will receive additional Alternate Directors).

[73] *See IMF Members' Quotas and Voting Power, and IMF Board of Governors*, INT'L MONETARY FUND (last visited Sept. 3, 2017), http://www.imf.org/external/np/sec/memdir/members.aspx (stating that Canada, France, Germany, United States, Italy, Japan, United Kingdom, China, Russia, and Saudia Arabia have a combined 1,312,437 votes out of the 2,517,646 total votes); *Group of Seven*, INFOPLEASE (last visited Sept. 3, 2017), http://www.infoplease.com/ce6/history/A0821954.html (listing the G7 countries as Canada, France, Germany, United States, Italy, Japan, United Kingdom).

"Most predominant states have been active forces behind the development of international law, and they have made extensive use of the international legal order to stabilize and improve their position."[74] The World Bank has experienced the same sort of criticisms. Notwithstanding these criticisms, and seeking more influence on the institution, developed and large emerging economies are asserting pressure on the World Bank.[75] Recently, the World Bank sought to pursue a reform program in which developing countries would get at least forty-seven percent of the voting shares in the institution, although fifty percent has been argued to be the optimal percentage.[76]

That being pursued, the voting structure still results in unfair situations. For example, the World Bank granted a loan on the condition that a country's water and sanitation services are privatized.[77] The country then sells its water and sanitation industries to a private consortium, which is financed by the IFC, a branch of the World Bank.[78] When the people of the country start complaining about sharp price increases due to privatization, the country is forced to turn to the IC-

---

[74] *See, e.g.,* Nico Kirsch, International Law in Times of Hegemony: Unequal Power and the Shaping of the International Legal Order, 16 EUR. J. INT'L L. 369, 382 (2005).

[75] Madeline Baer, *Water Privatization and Civil Society in Bolivia, Addressing the Democratic Deficit of International Organizations, Annual Meeting of International Studies Association,* ALL ACADEMIC RESEARCH (Mar. 24, 2006),
http://citation.allacademic.com//meta/p_mla_apa_research_citation/1/0/0/4/0/pages10040
8/p100408-1.php (providing another critique which charges that recent BWI' globalization policies favoring privatization—allowing private lenders to come in and charge higher rates—are further aggravating the problem for developing countries); *see Press Release, The World Bank, World Bank Reforming to Meet New Challenges, Zoellick Says,* THE WORLD BANK, (Oct. 6, 2009), http://go.worldbank.org/5JYWTSK5U0.

[76] *Id.* (discussing a speech made by World Bank Group President Robert B. Zoellick at the beginning of the 2009 Annual Meetings of the World Bank and IMF in Istanbul, Turkey). The World Bank's shareholders supported giving developing countries at least a 47 percent share of the voting shares, yet Zoellick called for developing countries to have a 50% share. *Id.; see* Robert B. Zoellick, President, The World Bank Group, Remarks at Board of Governors of World Bank Group Annual Meeting: The World Bank Group Beyond the Crisis (Oct. 6, 2009) (discussing the World Bank's pursuit of an ambitious program of reform).

[77] *See* ERIC TOUSSAINT, THE WORLD BANK A CRITICAL PRIMER 3 (Sylvain Dropsy ed., Elizabeth Anne trans., 2008).

[78] *Id.*

SID, a branch of the World Bank, to dispute the situation.[79] So the weighted voting structure allows larger countries to impose their policies through the World Bank, which in this scenario results in the World Bank Group controlling the (1) conditions for which a country may take a loan, (2) the financing for the privatization of certain services, and (3) the dispute settlement.[80] This scenario happened at El Alto (Bolivia) in 2004–05.[81]

Although reforms to promote good governance were stressed as early as 1996,[82] the IMF's governance did not begin a major reform process until 2006.[83] A 2009 Committee on IMF's Governance Reform report

---

[79] *Id.* at 3–4.

[80] *See id.*

[81] *Id.; see* Maude Barlow, *Securing the Right to Water in Bolivia,* BLUE PLANET PROJECT (Mar. 23, 2010) https://www.blueplanetproject.net/index.php/securing-the-right-to-water-in-bolivia/. "[C]itizens in El Alto, Bolivia [struggled] to regain control of their local water supply from multinational corporate giant, Suez. . . . As a condition for a World Bank loan, the public water system in El Alto was privatized in 1997. Eight years later, despite promises of expanded water services, the private company Aguas del Illimani (Suez is the major shareholder) had failed to deliver water to 200,000 people in El Alto and had no plans to do so in the future. . . . In January 2005, after a general strike and public protests demanding the immediate withdrawal of Suez from Bolivia and for the government to investigate the company's actions, the Bolivian government decided to cancel its contract with Aguas del Illimani. . . . Despite this initial victory, the Bolivian government, under pressure from the Inter–American Development Bank, the World Bank and German Corporation GTZ, announced its intention to create a supposed 'New Model' of Public–Private Partnership where Suez would continue to hold 35% of the shares." *Id.*

[82] *See* INT'L BANK FOR RECONSTRUCTION AND DEV., THE WORLD BANK PARTICIPATION SOURCEBOOK (The International Bank, 1996), http://documents.worldbank.org/curated/en/289471468741587739/pdf/multi-page.pdf (showing reform ideas proposed in 1996, which suggested that increased participation by developing countries was necessary).

[83] *See Governance Structure,* INT'L MONETARY FUND (last visited Sept. 3, 2017), http://www.imf.org/external/about/govstruct.htm (explaining the governance reform ideals between 2006 and 2008). A committee was appointed to assess the adequacy of the IMF's current framework. *Id.* The committee on IMF Governance Reform was appointed by Managing Director Dominique Strauss–Kahn on September 4, 2008. *Id.; see* INT'L MONETARY FUND, COMMITTEE ON IMF GOVERNANCE REFORM FINAL REPORT (Mar. 24, 2009), http://www.imf.org/external/np/omd/2009/govref/032409.pdf [hereinafter "COMMITTEE ON IMF"] (explaining the findings of the committee); *Press Release, Int'l Monetary Fund, IMF Managing Director Dominique Strauss–Kahn Welcomes Experts' Report on Fund Decision Making,* INTERNATIONAL MONETARY FUND (Mar. 25, 2009), http://www.imf.org/external/np/sec/pr/2009/pr0988.htm.

described the drawbacks of the current governance framework: legitimacy and effectiveness; political voice; the executive board itself; overlaps and gaps; and mandates.[84] To rectify the drawbacks, the Committee recommended enhancement of clear leadership, enablement of effective executive decision-making, and an increase in membership accountability.[85] Emerging economies are not in favor of the reforms sought by the IMF.[86]

The World Bank's governance, in its role as the premier multilateral banking institution and as the sole global institution of its sort, has been critiqued.[87] As a result of weathering the heavy criticism, the

---

[84] *See* COMMITTEE ON IMF, *supra* note 83, at 7–10. Changes are reforms that are implemented and take years to go into effect, and many nations are not following through with their respective portions of the bargain. *Id.* at 7. "High–level political representation on a decision–making body that provides strategic and policy direction, and discusses macroeconomic and financial policy coordination, is needed." *Id.* at 9. The Executive Board, while in actuality is a body of high professional and technical capacity, is treated by its members as a position on international civil servitude, rather than a capacity of political representation, therefore the members are often removed from the actual policy–making. *Id.* Regarding the overlaps and gaps, in order for a governing body to be efficient there needs to be clarity in the roles and responsibilities delineated to each area of the governmental framework. *Id.* "Components of institutional decision–making—namely, the legislative function, the executive function, and a means of measuring performance and holding the executive accountable—are insufficiently delineated and assigned. The IMFC lacks the mandate to take strategic decisions; the Board is too stretched in day–to–day operational decisions to be able to set broad strategic directions; and there are few explicit systems for measuring management and board performance and holding them accountable." *Id.*
[85] COMMITTEE ON IMF, *supra* note 83, at 10.
[86] *See* Lesley Wroughton, *Emerging nations stand firm on IMF vote reform*, REUTERS NEWS, Aug. 5, 2009 (explaining that emerging economies want voting shares realigned before governance reforms are tackled). Emerging powers want voting shares to reflect their shares within the global economies before the governance is reformed because the emerging economies fear that a decision–making ministerial council backed by the current IMF's powers would delay basic reforms emerging countries want. *Id.*
[87] Ngaire Woods, *The Challenge of Good Governance for the IMF and the World Bank Themselves*, World Development (May 2000) 17–8 (discussing the critiques as the greater influence in research direction and results by large shareholders, and the World Bank's Anglo–Saxon approach to economics including the homogeneity in the World Bank's staffing). An example of influence is that in the 1980's, the Reagan administration, Germans, and British played a role in squelching research on debt issues. *Id.* The Anglo–Saxon approach consisted of the staffing of the agency being dominated by English speaking

World Bank has evolved vastly since its inception and has become a pioneer in terms of accountability.[88] The World Bank's governance structure is in a constant state of review and reformation.[89] As such, the World Bank instituted an independent review by experienced individuals, which the World Bank hopes will aid in strengthening its aims of becoming more accountable, agile, effective, inclusive, innovative, and financially sound.[90]

That independent review, headed by former Mexican President Ernesto Zedillo, emphasized the lack of accountability at the top--at the level of the Executive Board and Senior Management.[91] The accountability problem is exasperated by the Executive Board having three counter-

---

United States' citizens. *Id.* Fluency in English advanced employees within the organization. *Id.*

[88] *Id.* at 6. In 1993, the World Bank became the first multilateral organization to create an independent inspection panel for public accountability. By 1998, that panel had received thirteen requests for inspection. *Id.*

[89] *See Press Release, The World Bank, Outside Review Supports World Bank Group Reform,* THE WORLD BANK (Oct. 21, 2009), http://go.worldbank.org/2I98FYWNJ0 (explaining that the reforms that are already underway deal with financial capacity, the strengthening of management accountability, the leadership selection process, expanding voice, and the restructure of the World Bank's governing bodies). Financial measures such as the injection of paid–in capital were developed to reform financial capacity. *Id.* The World Bank is doing an institutional review of independent evaluation entities to strengthen management accountability. *Id.* The leadership selection process was reformed so selection of the World Bank Group President is now merit–based, transparent, and open. *Id.* The World Bank's voice has been expanded through a new chair for Sub–Saharan Africa, an increase in developing countries' shares in IBRD, and a raise in developing and transition countries' voting power. *Id.* The World Bank Group's governing bodies were restructured to improve Board operations and client services. *Id.*

[90] *See Press Release, The World Bank, World Bank Reforming to Meet New Challenges, Zoellick Says, supra* note 75 (explaining that World Bank Group President Robert B. Zoellick created the High Level Commission on Modernization of World Bank Group Governance in October 2008, which did an external review of the World Bank Group's governance). Headed by former Mexican President Ernesto Zedillo, the Commission made five recommendations: 1) restructure the World Bank Group's governing bodies; 2) strengthen the World Bank Group's resource base; 3) strengthen management accountability; 4) reform the leadership selection process; and 5) enhance voice and participation. *Id.*

[91] *See* ZEDILLO COMM'N, REPOWERING THE WORLD BANK FOR THE 21ST CENTURY, REPORT OF THE HIGH–LEVEL COMMISSION ON MODERNIZATION OF WORLD BANK GROUP GOVERNANCE 30 (Oct. 20, 2009) [hereinafter "ZEDILLO COMM'N REPORT"], http://siteresources.worldbank.org/NEWS/Resources/WBGovernanceCOMMISSIONREPORT.pdf.

productive functions: political representation, management, and over-sight.[92] The report calls for more division of labor and responsibilities via a restructure of the current governance structure.[93] It is suggested that the Board of Directors be elevated to a "World Bank Board" with more responsibilities, including making major policy decisions, con-ducting general oversight of the institution, and approving the World Bank Group's overall strategy and direction.[94] Further, all responsibil-ity for the approval of all World Bank Group financing operations should be transferred to Management.[95] The separation of manage-ment responsibilities will provide a checks and balances system that will hold management accountable through effective performance evaluation by the World Bank Board.[96]

The need for reform in the BWI is evident by the recent creation of the Asian Infrastructure Investment Bank ("AIIB").[97] The AIIB is primarily focused on financing infrastructure, and it is the first multilateral de-velopment bank since the European Bank for Reconstruction and De-velopment was established in 1991.[98] China is the primary backer of the

---

[92] *Id.; Governing Structure of the World Bank*, THE WORLD BANK, http://web.worldbank.org/WBSITE/EXTERNAL/TOPICS/CSO/0,,contentMDK:20094705~ menuPK:220464~pagePK:220503~piPK:220476~theSitePK:228717,00.html (last visited Sept. 3, 2017).

[93] *See* ZEDILLO COMM'N REPORT, *supra* note 91, at 30, 39.

[94] *See id.* at 39.

[95] *See id.* at 40.

[96] *See id.* at 43.

[97] *See* Sue-Lin Wong, *China launches new AIIB development bank as power balance shifts*, REU-TERS.COM (last visited Sept. 3, 2017), http://www.reuters.com/article/us-asia-aiib-investment-idUSKCN0UU03Y, (reporting on the inauguration of the bank by Chinese President Xi Jinping, and the lending requirements the bank will demand as a condition of the loans). The AIIB "will not force borrowers to adopt the kind of free-market prac-tices favored by the IMF," and the bank hopes that this measure will help it "avoid the criticism leveled against its rivals, which some say impose unreasonable demands on borrowers." *Id.*

[98] *See Focus Areas*, AIIB.ORG (last visited Sept. 3, 2017), https://www.aiib.org/en/about-aiib/who-we-are/our-work/index.html (outlining the main infrastructure areas that the AIIB hope to emphasize). The main areas of emphasis include Rural Infrastructure and Agricultural Development, Energy and Power, Environmental Protection, Transportation and Telecommunication, Water Supply and Sanitation, and Urban Development and Logistics. *Id. See also* Sara Hsu, *How China's Asian Infrastructure Investment Bank Fared Its*

AIIB, with an individual capital contribution of almost thirty billion dollars of the bank's initial total capital assets of one-hundred billion dollars.[99] The main reasons for China's aggressive entry into multilateral infrastructure lending include the sluggish pace of the BWI in reforming their "representational and operational structures."[100] Others argue that China's aim is to challenge the Washington Consensus[101] inherent within the BWI, by advancing a new Beijing Consensus[102] through the AIIB.[103]

First Year, FORBES.COM (last visited Sept. 3, 2017), https://www.forbes.com/sites/sarahsu/2017/01/14/how-chinas-asian-infrastructure-investment-bank-fared-its-first-year/#752267f35a7f (providing a comprehensive analysis of the results from the first year of operation of AIIB). In its first year of operation, the AIIB invested in nine total projects, including loans for $165 million in Bangladesh, "a $216.5 million loan for a National Slum Upgrading Project in Indonesia, a $27.5 million loan for the Dushanbe-Uzbekistan Border Road Improvement Project in Tajikistan, and a $100 million loan for the Shorkot-Khanewal Section of National Motorway M-4 in Pakistan." *Id.* The AIIB, which is managed by Jin Liquin, who has previously worked with the World Bank, has been a resounding success because China is using the goodwill gained from facilitating these and other loans to advance its "soft power, [and expand] its economic interests while gaining acceptance on the world stage." *Id.*

[99] *See* Gregory T. Chin, *Asian Infrastructure Investment Bank: Governance Innovation and Prospects Global Governance* 22 GLOB. GOVERNANCE 11 (2016) (providing an analysis of the governance innovations undertaken by the AIIB and its future potential).

[100] *Id* at 11; *see also* Rebecca Liao, *Out of the Bretton Woods--How the AIIB is Different*, LINN-BENTON.EDU (July 27, 2015) http://cf.linnbenton.edu/artcom/social_science/clarkd/upload/Out%20of%20the%20Bretton%20Woods.pdf (stating the voting structure at the BWI "between advanced and developing economies is still split at around 60–40, and Washington's voting bloc has remained constant at around 17 percent, even though 73 percent of developing countries have grown faster than the U.S. since the 1990s, to the tune of 3.3 percent a year.").

[101] *See* LI Tao, et al., *Implication of the Asian Infrastructure Investment Bank for Global Financial Governance: Accommodation or Confrontation?* 9 TSINGHUA CHINA L. REV. 139 (2016); *see also* Daniel C.K Chow, *Why China Established the Asia Infrastructure Investment Bank*, 49 VAND. J. TRANSNAT'L L. 1255 (2016). The Washington Consensus is a set of principles that include fiscal discipline, tax reform, trade liberalization, deregulation, and unfeather access for foreign direct investment. *Id.*

[102] *See Id.* The Beijing Consensus follows a doctrine of non-interference and non-conditionality. *Id.* Additionally, it aims to promote China's state owned enterprises and the Renminbi as an international currency. *Id.*

[103] *See* Robert Wihtol, *Beijing's Challenge to the Global Financial Architecture*, GEO. J. OF ASIAN AFF., (Spring 2015).

The BWI can learn valuable lessons from the emergence of the AIIB. First, the AIIB is organized in a decentralized structure that aims to reduce expenses and preserve local interests by having a nonresident executive board that can communicate electronically.[104] Nonresident executive boards, originally advanced by John Maynard Keynes, can be successful in alleviating the perception that the BWI are subservient to a Washington Consensus.[105] Second, the World Bank and the IMF must reform their representational and organizational structures to prevent other multilateral development banks from competing against them while using unsustainable environmental and social standards that are different from the more stringent norms advanced by the BWI.

To illustrate, the AIIB recently agreed to finance an Indonesian Coal Power Plant that the World Bank had previously declined to fund.[106] The AIIB and similar future multilateral development banks are existential threats to the BWI because they do not require neoliberal economic reforms or sustainable environmental and social policies as a condition of securing development loans.

---

[104] *See* Chin, *supra* note 99 (outlining the new innovations that the AIIB has undertaken to reduce costs and improve operations).

[105] Leonardo Martinez-Diaz, *Executive Boards in International Organizations: Lessons for Strengthening IMF Governance*, THE BROOKINGS INSTITUTION (last visited Sept. 3, 2017), http://www.ieo-imf.org/ieo/files/completedevaluations/05212008BP08_08.pdf (providing a comparative study on the effectiveness of other institutions in organizing non-resident boards).

[106] *See* Chow, *supra* note 101 (detailing how the AIIB has already pre-approved an Indonesia coal-power plant that the World Bank would not approve due to its "harmful environmental impact."); Edward Wong, *Glut of Coal Powered Plants Casts Doubt on China's Energy Priorities*, N.Y. TIMES (last visited Sept. 3, 2017), http://www.nytimes.com/2015/11/12/world/asia/china-coal-power-energy-policy.html?_r=0 [https:/perma.cc/J3G7-7FPX (reporting on China's commitment to new coal powered plants). *But see* Kevin Frayer, *We will not invest in coal, says China's would-be World Bank*, THE TIMES (last visited Sept. 3, 2017), https://www.thetimes.co.uk/article/we-will-not-invest-in-coal-says-chinas-would-be-world-bank-g2n7jntx7 (providing details on the AIIB's new policy of staying away from investments in coal power plants). "The Asian Infrastructure Investment Bank has promised to avoid financing coalmines and power stations." *Id.*

These unrestricted loans are particularly attractive to developing nations that usually must make some concessions (many of which are unfavorable in the long term) when attempting to secure a loan from the World Bank.[107]

---

[107] *See* Chow, *supra* note 101. The Indonesian loan illustrates the attractiveness of the AIIB. *See id.* When commenting on the new loan for the coal power plant, the Indonesian government said that the "AIIB imposes looser environment requirement[s] in disbursing its loans, making it the preferred creditor for financing Indonesia's coal-fired power plant projects." *See id.*

3

NEOLIBERALISM

ON A GLOBAL SCALE

T his chapter provides an overview of the economic principles which have controlled the actions of the BWI and World Trade Organizations, and to show how these principles have led to the failure of these institutions. The first subsection suggests that specific economic policies have played a fundamental role in the outcome of implementing the ideals underlying the BWI.[1] The second subsection presents the evolution of Neoliberalism and how it has had dramatic negative effects on the global economy throughout the last two centuries.[2] The third subsection analyzes the IMF and the World Bank's use of loan conditions, their chosen tool for imposing Neoliberalism.[3]

Influence through Vote & Governance

Through the looking glass of the Great Depression, the IMF and the World Bank's policies were based primarily on Keynes' prescriptions to resolve global economic problems.[4] However, by the mid 1980's, the controlling economic policy of these institutions shifted to the neoclas-

---

[1] *See infra* Chapter III.A.
[2] *See infra* Chapter III.B.
[3] *See infra* Chapter III.C.
[4] *See* STIGLITZ, *supra* Chapter I note 2, at 11.

sical approach.[5] "The Keynesian orientation of the IMF, which emphasized market failures and the role for government in job creation, was
replaced by the free market mantra of the 1980's, as part of a new
"Washington Consensus"-- a consensus between the IMF, the World
Bank, and the U.S. Treasury about the "right" policies for developing
countries -- that signaled a radically different approach to economic
development and stabilization."[6] Rapid trade liberalization corresponding to free market ideology would ultimately lead to the colonization of developing countries to the IMF.[7]

The IMF brought in the World Bank, initially planning to provide bil-
lions of dollars in emergency support to Europe after the fall of the Berlin Wall.[8] In the 1980's the Bank lost sight of this humanitarian foundation and began lending structural adjustment loans burdened with IMF
imposed conditions to developing countries.[9] The BWI collectively
represented the aggregate desire of the capitalist market to expand
globally beyond the boundaries of the developed industrial world with
minimum state restrictions.[10] Within the IMF, capitalistic nations like

---

[5] See ARIEL BUIRA, THE IMF AND THE WORLD BANK AT SIXTY 8 (2005) ("The growing breach
between world economic and financial realities and the governance structure of the BWI
argues for reform to enhance the legitimacy and restore the effectiveness of these institutions").

[6] See STIGLITZ, supra Chapter I note 2, at 16.

[7] See id.

[8] See id. at 14.

[9] See CARL JAYARAJAH & WILLIAM H. BRANSON, OPERATIONS EVALUATION DEP'T, STRUC-
TURAL & SECTORAL ADJUSTMENT: WORLD BANK EXPERIENCE, 1980–92 The World Bank,
1995) (explaining an extensive study performed by the Operations Evaluation Department in 1995 regarding the World Bank's experience with adjustment lending in the
1980's, including conditionality).

[10] See BUIRA, supra Chapter II note 63, at 8. Under Bretton Woods, structural balance of
payments disequilibria were to be corrected by exchange rate movements. Id. The IMF
through its surveillance function is supposed to assess a country's economic health by
reviewing its monetary, fiscal, exchange rate, trade and other financial policies. Id.
However, under Milton Friedman's floating exchange rate approach, developed countries would essentially absolve themselves from any form of IMF oversight. See MILTON
FRIEDMAN, CAPITALISM AND FREEDOM, 65–71 (2nd ed. 1982); John R. Kroger, Enron, Fraud,
and Securities Reform: An Enron Prosecutor's Perspective, 76. U. COLO. L. REV. 57, 60–65
(2005) (stating there is a complete lack of transparency and review of leading internation-

the United States and England forcibly imposed neoliberal ideologies on underdeveloped countries by swinging heavily weighted voting power in favor of free markets.[11] President Reagan brought this neoliberal ideal to the annual meeting of the World Bank in 1983 when he stated:

"The societies that achieved the most spectacular, broad based economic progress in the shortest period of time have not been the biggest in size, nor the richest in resources and certainly not the most rigidly controlled. What has united them all was their belief in the magic of the marketplace. Millions of individuals making their own decisions in the marketplace will always allocate resources better than any centralized government planning process."[12]

The IMF was the perfect mechanism for the United States to realistically pursue an implementation of the free-market concept on a global scale.[13] Starting in the mid 1970's, the IMF and the World Bank hired graduates from the Chicago School to implement capitalistic free market ideals, irrespective of humanitarian rights.[14] Underdeveloped countries which had sought refuge in the IMF and World Bank were blindly subjected to the neoliberal ideas of the Chicago School and became heavily indebted to the institutions.[15]

---

al financial bodies promotes lack of discretion, illegality, and fraud within the global economic community).

[11] *See* STIGLITZ, *supra* Chapter 1, note 2, at 14–15. The IMF and the World Bank were both driven by the collective will of the G-7, the governments of the most important advanced industrial countries. *Id.* These countries are the United States, Japan, Germany, Canada, Italy, United Kingdom and France. *Id.* In year 2011 the G-8 was formed to include Russia. *Id.*

[12] *See* RICHARD PEET, UNHOLY TRINITY: THE IMF, WORLD BANK, AND WTO 13 (2003) (recognizing that Friedman and the Austrian School of Economics had profound implications on global fiscal policy).

[13] *See generally* NAOMI KLEIN, THE SHOCK DOCTRINE: THE RISE OF DISASTER CAPITALISM 388–403 (Random House Of Canada, 2007).

[14] *Id.* at 161–63 (describing the policy makers of the IMF and their relation to the Chicago School).

[15] *See generally id.* at 388–403 (building a connection between lifting regulations on interest rates and the colonization of Third World countries).

The IMF issued structural adjustment programs to bail out countries in financial crisis, which also helped to advance privatization and free trade.[16] Countries that adhered to the adjustment programs took on massive floating interest rate loans.[17] Since interest rates were not regulated under the IMF and World Bank,[18] eventually the cost of borrowing money increased at a faster pace than countries could repay debt. This morally bankrupt lending practice was the driving force behind the IMF's and World Bank's colonization of financially bankrupt countries.[19]

Evolution & Critique of Neoliberalism

Prior to examining Neoliberalism's impact on the policies of the IMF and World Bank, it is worth discussing the evolution of political economics. Keynesian economics became most popular when government regulations were desired.[20] From the Great Depression until the end of

---

[16] *Id.* at 155–56, 200–03, 216. The IMF was originally concerned with exchange rates and balance of payment loans. *Id.* The IMF short term loans were at first used mainly by the same circle of industrial economies that had dominated the institution's founding. *See* KLEIN, *supra* note 15, at 155–56, 200–03, 216. The IMF shifted in the mid 1970's to a more intervention-type stance where loans were granted under conditions of greater austerity to Third World countries. *Id.* Loan conditionality was based on how countries achieve economic growth. *Id.* This conception was formulated by right wing politicians and bureaucrats operating mainly through the U.S. Treasury in the series of Republican administrations. *Id.* The result of neoliberal conditionality, together with policy moves, such as capital account liberalization, has proven to be disastrous for working people in developing countries. *Id.*

[17] *See generally* KLEIN, *supra* note 15, at 156 (discussing the issues pertaining to government debt inheritance).

[18] *See* BUIRA, *supra* Chapter II note 63, at 72 (stating that Ronald Reagan and Margaret Thatcher had a policy to promote free market reform and opened the developing world to foreign trade and investment).

[19] *See* STIGLITZ, *supra* Chapter I note 2, at 41 (stating that the Fund's approach to developing countries has had the feel of a colonial ruler; KLEIN, *supra* note 15 (explaining that industrialized countries pillage Third World countries in the modern day just as governments colonized the New World in the pre-industrialization era).

[20] *See* PAUL KRUGMAN, THE RETURN OF DEPRESSION ON ECONOMICS AND THE CRISIS OF 2008 100 (W. W. Norton & Company, 2009) (explaining how during the 1930s the United States fell into the Great Depression and John Maynard Keynes attempted to explain the causes of the slump to the general public).

World War II, Keynesian economics had its primary influences on economic policies.[21] Keynes presumed that in order to correct market imperfections, state intervention had to be implemented. [22] One of Keynes' most important lessons was that markets are not self-correcting and government intervention is required to ensure recovery and a return to full employment.[23]

Keynesian economics lost popularity in the mid-1970's due to stagflation and associated ideological assaults launched by the Chicago School.[24] Unlike Keynes' idealization of government regulations, economists from the Chicago School, such as Milton Friedman, perceived most government expenditures as excessive. Hence, government intervention was viewed as inefficient and not likely to achieve projected goals.[25]

With Friedman's help, the Chicago School derived a three-part formula for creating the perfect free market economy.[26] The formula included

---

[21] See id. at 102 (expounding on the notion that Keynes was in favor of macroeconomic intervention and this was viewed as acceptable by conservatives throughout WWII).

[22] See id. (making an assumption that Keynes did not want to return to a free market ideal even after the economy responded positively to government intervention).

[23] See JOSEPH E. STIGLITZ, THE STIGLITZ REPORT: Reforming the International Monetary and Financial 20 (2010) (explaining how the United States economy would not have recovered after Great Depression without government intervention).

[24] See BEN FINE, ECONOMICS IMPERIALISM AND INTELLECTUAL PROGRESS, HISTORY OF ECONOMICS REVIEW 15 (2000). The cornerstone of Milton Friedman's economic theory was that individuals make economic choices based upon self-interests alone, and therefore, rational expectations of individuals in the market cannot be predicted through quantitative data. See id. Optimal levels of economic health were measured and predicted by formulating the rational expectations of individuals. Id. Friedman's rational expectations theory did not simulate a systematic macroeconomic policy requiring the gathering of data to calculate economic agents. Id.

[25] See STIGLITZ, supra Chapter I note 2, at 60 (discussing the economic policies behind the global financial crisis of 2008 and mentioning how doctrines that supported deregulation were predicated on the assumption that sophisticated market participants were rational and had rational expectations and unfettered markets would result in optimal economic efficiency).

[26] See FRIEDMAN, supra note 12, at 65–71. Friedman promoted a floating exchange rate system because it is self-correcting and fully automatic. Id. Friedman believed the instability of exchange rates is a symptom of instability in the underlying economic structure. Id. Elimination of this symptom by administrative freezing of exchange rates, a method

government deregulation, privatization of government enterprises, and cutbacks on government spending.[27] Under this doctrine, only self-regulation was appropriate.[28] To increase overall wealth, the government would have to not only sell all state capital assets to private corporations, but also dramatically cut back entitlements, minimal taxes, and trade deregulation.[29]

In the late twentieth century, the Chicago School began to have a profound influence on South American Governments, such as Chile.[30] At this time, Chile was under the power of a socialist group led by Salvador Allende ("Allende").[31] Allende came into power as a result of an election in which he promised to promote a democratic society.[32]

---

of direct controls, only aggravates the underlying problem. *Id.* One way to correct this problem is for the U.S. to announce that it will not proclaim official exchange rates between the dollar and other currencies, and in addition, it will not engage in any speculative or other activities influencing exchange rates. *Id.* Exchange rates would then be determined in free markets. *Id.* These measures would conflict with the U.S. obligation to the IMF, to specify an official parity for the dollar. *See* FRIEDMAN, *supra* note 12, at 65–71. However, the IMF found it possible to reconcile Canada's failure to specify a parity with its Articles and gave its approval to a floating rate for Canada. *Id.* The IMF should do the same for the U.S. *Id.* Also, other nations will be able to peg their currency to the U.S. by drawing on reserves, coordinating their internal policies with U.S. policy, and by tightening or loosening direct controls on trade. *Id.*

[27] *See id.* (speaking on the pitfalls of social welfare programs and government regulations; for example, minimum wage laws effectively increase the unemployment rate because employers cannot afford to pay workers at the required rates). *But see* Frontline: The Warning (PBS DVD release Jan. 5, 2010) (showing that Summers, the Obama's administration financial advisor, is unopposed to government regulation).

[28] *See* STIGLITZ, *supra* Chapter I note 2, at 60 (discussing the doctrines which support free markets).

[29] *See* Kroger, *supra* note 12, at 57, 60 (exemplifying the consequences of complete government deregulation; Enron was built upon deregulation).

[30] *See e.g.*, NOAM CHOMSKY, PROFIT OVER PEOPLE: NEOLIBERALISM & GLOBAL ORDER 9 (2003); *see also* BUIRA, *supra* Chapter II note 63, at 145 (during the 1990's, policymakers in Chile sought to improve investor confidence and promote stable, sustainable economic and export growth. Chile confronted issues resulting from the neoliberal hyperinflation with Capital Management Techniques "CMTs". The CMT Chile set in place in the 1990's was designed to insulate the economy from volatile international capital flows).

[31] *See e.g.*, BUIRA, *supra* Chapter II, note 63. Friedman had no qualms over the military overthrow of Chile's democratically elected Allende government in 1973, because Allende was interfering with business control of Chilean society. *Id.* After fifteen years of often brutal and savage dictatorship—all in the name of the democratic free market—

Succeeding Allende, Augusto Pinochet and his military tried to increase the overall wealth of the Chilean economy.[33] However, inflation doubled in the first eight or nine months of the new regime.[34] When rates of inflation continued to rise, Pinochet consulted with economists to stabilize the failed economy.[35] These economists were called the "Chicago Boys" because they received their Ph.D. degrees at the University of Chicago.[36] At the time, the "Chicago Boys" was the only group of economists in Chile not tainted by a connection with the Allende socialists.[37] They were "untainted" because the University of Chicago was among the few institutions in the United States where the economics department had a strong group of free-market economists.[38]

---

formal democracy was restored in 1989 with a constitution that made it vastly more difficult, if not impossible, for the citizenry to challenge the business–military domination of Chilean society. *Id.; see also* KLEIN, *supra* note 15, at 97 (explaining how Sergio de Castro was a prominent Chilean U.S. trained economist); *see id.* at 18, 82 (defining the trinity of free markets as privatization, deregulation, and cuts of social spending).

[32] *See* BUIRA, *supra* Chapter II, note 63, at 145 (explaining how Chile uses CMT's to protect their economic infrastructures which were derailed during the 1970's and 1980's when the Chicago School had profound influences on their financial stability). "The policy regime sought to balance the challenges and opportunities of financial integration, lengthen the maturity structure and stabilize capital inflows, mitigate the effect of large volumes of inflow on the currency and exports, and protect the economy from the instability associated with speculative excess and the sudden withdrawal of external finance." *Id.*

[33] *See* BUIRA, *supra* Chapter II note 63, at 147 (showing how CMT's greatly reduced the likelihood that the currency would appreciate and made it difficult for investors to leave, which would ultimately jeopardize the Chilean currency).

[34] *See id.* (showing that despite restraints on trade, investors committed funds to the Chilean infrastructure because the regime offered attractive opportunities for development within their growing market).

[35] *See id.* at 151 (Ariel Buira and the G24 Research Program 2003) (explaining how the CMTs employed in Chile in the 1990s not only reduced the risk of financial crisis but was a major preventative defense against IMF involvement within their policymaking).

[36] *See* KLEIN, *supra* note 14, at 71, 77–81 (describing the Chicago Boys influence on the Chilean government in the 1970's and 1980's).

[37] *See* BUIRA, *supra* Chapter II note 63, at 150. "The general soundness of the Chilean banking system in the 1990s and macroeconomic policy, the maintenance of price stability and the high level of official reserves were important sources of investor confidence." *Id.* at 145. "International support for the neoliberal aspects of Chile's economic reforms provided the government with the political space to experiment with CMTs." *Id.*

[38] *See* KLEIN, *supra* note 15, at 75 (explaining how the Chicago School influenced the theory taught within the Chilean economic schools).

The Chicago Boys assured Pinochet that if he withdrew government involvement from all private sectors at once, the natural laws of economics would push the domestic economic variables, such as inflation and unemployment, back to equilibrium.[39] Pinochet followed the Chicago School's recommendations; he privatized a majority of state-owned companies (including several banks), permitted speculative financing of projects, opened borders to foreign imports exposing Chilean manufacturers to competition, and cut all government funding by ten percent.[40] In 1974, Pinochet's adaptations backfired and inflation escalated above 700 percent.[41] Scholars of the Chicago School insisted that the inflation was attributable to Pinochet's incorrect implementation of free market ideals.[42] Noam Chomsky articulated the concerns of Henry Kissinger regarding the likelihood of a widespread negative implication of Pinochet's regime.[43] Chomsky described the implications of the Chilean economic practices as a true threat to social change worldwide.[44]

Within a year, Friedman convinced Pinochet to fire his economic advisor and hire Sergio de Castro as the finance minister.[45] Castro invited friends from the Chicago School to join him in the Chilean government,

---

[39] See FRIEDMAN, *supra* note 12, at 15 (explaining how Neoliberalism is the cure to economic inefficiencies).

[40] See KLEIN, *supra* note 15, at 75–100 (stating that Pinochet was an admired Chilean leader, and defining the trinity of free markets as privatization, deregulation, and cuts of social spending).

[41] See *Inflation Chile 1974*, INFLATION.EU (last visited Sept. 1, 2017), http://www.inflation.eu/inflation-rates/chile/historic-inflation/cpi-inflation-chile-1974.aspx.

[42] See *id.* at 75–80 (explaining how the Chicago Boys influenced Chilean economic policy).

[43] See CHOMSKY, *supra* note 32, at 21–2. Noam Chomsky is the leading intellectual figure in the world today in the battle for democracy and against Neoliberalism. *Id.* at 11. In the 1960's, Chomsky was a prominent U.S. critic of the Vietnam war, and, more broadly, he became perhaps the most trenchant analyst of the ways U.S. foreign policy undermines democracy, quashes human rights, and promotes the interests of the wealthy few. *Id.* In the 1970's, Chomsky, along with his co-author Edward S. Herman, began their research on how the U.S news media serves elite interests and undermines the capacity of the citizenry to actually rule their lives in a democratic fashion. *Id.* at 11.

[44] See *id.* (describing the issues of Chile in light of neoliberal influence).

[45] See KLEIN, *supra* note 14, at 75.

and he appointed one of the Chicago School economists to the central bank.[46] In 1975, over 500 companies were privatized, government spending was cut by twenty seven percent, domestic manufacturers were absolved, and the Chilean economy fell into a major recession.[47] Friedman's concept of shocking the economy into equilibrium by lifting all government restraints on trade had failed to cure Chile's domestic economic market problems.[48]

Certain governments, such as Mexico, have begun to view Chile as a failed free market experiment and so realize the necessity to strengthen their financial systems through regulations.[49] But supporters of free markets, such as defenders of the Washington Consensus, continue to argue against any artificial barriers to trade.[50] The free market supporters continue to believe that growth can be achieved through sound budgets, low inflation, market deregulation, and free trade.[51]

Further magnifying the failure of Chile's economic policies was the success of countries that have moved away from the policies set forth by the "Washington Consensus." Brazil and Bolivia are two examples of

---

[46] See KLEIN, supra note 14, at 254–55 (explaining how the Chicago Boys sought to liberate central banks in Africa).
[47] See id.
[48] See id. at 75–100 (denoting how the Chicago Boy theory of economic policy did not have positive long lasting effects on the Chilean economy).
[49] See KRUGMAN, supra note 21, at 31–34 ("If a national economy goes sour and default looms, the IMF is the preferred creditor. It gets paid back first – even if others, such as foreign creditors, do not. They might get nothing. So a rational private sector financial institution is going to insist on a risk premium higher interest rate to cover the higher likelihood of not getting paid back."); see also STIGLITZ, supra Chapter 1, note 2, at 206.
[50] See KRUGMAN, supra note 21, at 31–34. Stiglitz, commenting on his experience at the World Bank and their failed policy decision making:
At the World Bank, during the time I was there, there was an increasing conviction that participation mattered, that policies and programs could to be imposed on countries but to be successful had to be "owned" by them, that consensus building was essential, that policies and development strategies had to be adapted to the situation in the country, that there should be a shift from "conditionality" to "selectivity", rewarding countries that had proved track records for using funds well with more funds, trusting them to continue to make good use of their funds, and providing them with strong incentives. Id.; see also STIGLITZ, supra Chapter 1 note 2, at 49.
[51] See KRUGMAN, supra note 21, at 31–4.

two South American economies that have challenged the neoliberal model and moved to a more nationalistic approach.[52]

Bolivia, like many other South American countries, was in the midst of a debt crisis at the start of the 1980s.[53] Fueled by increased public borrowing during the petrodollar boom of the 1970's and the corruption of the military governments, Bolivia's GDP declined every year between 1981–1986.[54] Pushed to the brink of insolvency from the falling price of tin, elections were held a year early.[55] Victor Paz Estenssoro's election marked the beginning of Neoliberalism in Bolivia.[56]

Paz Estenssoro, through Presidential Decree 21060, initiated the New Economic Policy (NEP), which called for the closing of state mines, privatized state-owned enterprises, and increased foreign direct investment--all leading to the end of protectionist policies that had been in place.[57] While the plan initially succeeded in slowing inflation within the first couple of weeks, over time it failed to address Bolivia's fundamental economic problems.[58] In 1993, under the presidency of Gonzalo Sánchez de Lozada, Bolivia instituted what is known as "El Plan de Todos."[59] The Law of Capitalization implemented the partial privat-

---

[52] *See* Nathaneal Hamilton, The Brazilian Economy in Transition: Explaining President Lula's Response to Neoliberal Reform (May 23, 2011) (unpublished M.A. dissertation, San Diego State University), http://sdsudspace.calstate.edu/bitstream/handle/10211.10/1351/Hamilton_Nathanael.pdf?sequence=1.

[53] *See* Lydia Chavez, *Man in the News; Bolivian in an Encore: Victor Paz Estenssoro*, THE N.Y. TIMES (Aug. 7, 1985), http://www.nytimes.com/1985/08/07/world/man-in-the-news-bolivian-in-an-encore-victor-paz-estenssoro.html.

[54] Benjamin Kohl, *Challenges to Neoliberal Homogenies in Bolivia*, ANTIPODE 304, 310 (2006), http://www.temple.edu/gus/kohl/documents/ChallengesNLHegAntipode.pdf.

[55] *Id.*

[56] *See* Chavez, *supra* note 54.

[57] *See* Kohl, *supra* note 55.

[58] *See id.* at 310–11.

[59] Benjamin Kohl, *Restructuring Citizenship in Bolivia: El Plan de Todos*, 27.2 INT'L J. URB. & REG'L RES. 337, 340 (2003).

ization of five major industries in Bolivia:[60] oil and gas, telecommunications, airlines, power generations, and railroads.[61] Bolivia, a 50 percent shareholder in the multinational corporations that took control of these industries, planned on using the stock revenue to bail out the failing national pension system; however, factors such as lost revenues resulting from the Law of Capitalization, as well as economic forecasts not being met, led to a major reduction of government programs.[62]

A populist backlash against neoliberal policies soon followed, culminating in the Cochabamba water protests of 2000 and the Bolivian gas conflict of 2003.[63] As a result, President Sánchez went into exile in the United States, and Evo Morales, a member of Bolivia's Aymara culture, became the country's first Native-American leader (a majority of whose population is Native American).

President Morales rejected Neoliberalism implemented state control over the national economy, as evidenced by the nationalization of the hydrocarbon sector, and developed national social-welfare programs.[64] The result seems to be a success for Bolivia. In 2010, the country's exports totaled $7.1 billion while imports totaled $5.3 billion, resulting in a healthy trade surplus of $1.6 billion.[65]

Bolivia is part of several international trade partnerships, including the Andean Community (the "CAN") and the Bolivarian Alliance for the Americas (the "ALBA").[66] The country currently enjoys a B+ rating from the Standards and Poor rating agency.[67] Though the country still

---

[60] *Id.* "El Plan de Todos" was not a complete transfer over of the public sector to private industry; rather, it was a sale of 50% of the state industries to multinational corporations. The remaining shares were transferred. *Id.*

[61] *Id.*

[62] *Id.*

[63] *See* Press Release, U.S. State Dep't, Background notes: Bolivia (Aug, 3, 2011).

[64] *Id.*

[65] *Id.*

[66] *Id.*

[67] *See Sovereign's Ratings List*, STANDARD AND POOR'S RATINGS SERVS. (last visited Sept. 1, 2017), http://www.standardandpoors.com/ratings/sovereigns/ratings-list/en/us/?subSectorCode=39&sectorId=1221186707758&subSectorId=1221187348494.

is heavily dependent on foreign assistance to help finance development projects,[68] Bolivia has rebounded nicely following its stint with Neoliberalism.

Brazil was another successful example of a country flourishing after moving away from externally imposed neoliberal economic policies. Neoliberal reform was brought to Brazil after the election of Fernando Collor de Mello in 1990.[69] The Collor de Mello administration implemented a number of policies to help deal with the high inflation rates of the 1990's, including market deregulation, reduction of import tariffs, and an investor–friendly tax system that helped pave the way to opening up Brazil to the global market.[70] A second round of neoliberal policies were implemented by the administration of Itamar Franco with the "Plano Real".[71] These measures involved a mix of privatizing several state-owned entities, including a global public offering of shares of the oil and gas giant Petrobas, and the raising of interest rates.[72] The plan drew a huge influx of foreign investors to Brazil.[73] Although the "Plano Real" at first seemed a success, it was not able to produce mass prosperity.[74]

Luiz Ignazio "Lula" Da Silva, former head of the metallurgical workers labor union, became the next President. Coming from his left-leaning Workers Party, he also had to deal with the conservative neoliberals.[75] Lula issued a statement during the 2002 campaign stating that his gov-

---

[68] *See* U.S. State Dep't, *supra* note 64.

[69] *See* James Brooke, *Man in the News; The Choice of Brazilians; Fernando Collor*, THE N.Y. TIMES (Dec. 20, 1989), http://www.nytimes.com/1989/12/20/world/man-in-the-news-the-choice-of-brazilians-fernando-collor.html.

[70] *See* Maria de Lourdes Rollemberg Mollo & Alfredo Saad-Filho, *Neoliberal Economic Policies in Brazil (1994–2005): Cardoso, Lula and the Need for a Democratic Alternative*, 11 NEW POL. ECON. 99 (2006).

[71] *Id.*

[72] *See* Hamilton, *supra* note 53.

[73] *See id.*

[74] *See Sovereign's Ratings List, supra* note 68.

[75] *See* Gerardo Renique, *Introduction: Latin America Today: The Revolt Against Neoliberalism*, 19 SOCIALISM AND DEMOCRACY 1, 1–11, 182 (2005).

ernment would respect the IMF program agreed upon by the Cardoso administration, and maintained interest rates at levels set out by the "Plano Real."[76] In stark contrast to these neoliberal measures, Lula introduced "Bolsa Familia," a government program aimed to help reduce poverty by providing a government subsidy to families whose children attend school.[77] The multidisciplinary approach used by Brazil is a reason for the economic success attained in the nation before the 2015 recession devastated the economy[78]

Amid the economic downturn of 2006, Brazil had managed to maintain strong economic activity,[79] until an investigation into business and political corruption that started in 2015, sent the South American economic power into a deep recession. [80] The state-run energy company, Petrobras, at the center of the corruption scandal, is still among the international industrial leaders in oil production.[81] A portion of government expenditures continues to be directed at a number of high-tech industries, including aerospace, information technology, and telecommunication.[82] Government willingness to invest in innovation has led to success in private entrepreneurship, resulting in a growing middle class that accounted for more than half of the 190 million people in

---

[76] *See* Hamilton, *supra* note 53.

[77] *See How to get children out of jobs and into school: The limits of Brazil's much admired and emulated anti-poverty programme*, ECONOMIST (July 29, 2010) http://www.economist.com/node/16690887 (last visited Apr. 11, 2017).

[78] Nick Moriff, *A Corruption Scandal wrecked Brazil's economy. Now, workers face the consequences*, THE WASHINGTON POST (Jun. 19, 2017), https://www.washingtonpost.com/world/the_americas/a-corruption-scandal-wrecked-brazils-economy-now-workers-face-the-consequences/2017/06/16/a2be0faa-505b-11e7-b74e-0d2785d3083d_story.html?utm_term=.a6bdb92bd5f5.

[79] *See* Andrew Downie & Tim Padgett, *The One Country That Might Avoid Recession...*, TIME (Mar. 05, 2009), http://www.time.com/time/magazine/article/0,9171,1883301-1,00.html.

[80] Jonathan Watts, *Operation Car Wash: Is this the biggest corruption scandal in history?*, THE GUARDIAN (June 1, 2017) https://www.theguardian.com/world/2017/jun/01/brazil-operation-car-wash-is-this-the-biggest-corruption-scandal-in-history.

[81] *See* Lori Ioannou, *Brazil's Start-up Generation*, TIME ONLINE (Aug. 22, 2010), http://www.time.com/time/magazine/article/0,9171,2010076,00.html.

[82] *See* Press Release, U.S. State Dep't, Background notes: Brazil (Mar, 8, 2011).

Brazil before the recession.[83] Signs point to the end of the Brazilian recession,[84] and the country, still rich with resources, is looking to benefit from added representation at the negotiating tables of the BWI.[85]

Loan Conditionality

The economic policies of those running the IMF and World Bank have generally been imposed through conditions placed on loans and other benefits of membership with the IMF and World Bank. The IMF's embrace of loan conditionality was declared the "biggest divergence from the Bretton Woods objectives."[86] The principle of conditionality was incorporated within the Articles of Agreement in 1969, empowering the IMF to condition access to financial assistance upon the borrowing country's assent to mandated reforms targeting primary causes of their balance of payments issues.[87] The majority of conditions imposed on

---

[83] *Id.*

[84] *Brazil - Economic forecast summary*, OECD (Oct. 23, 2017) http://www.oecd.org/eco/outlook/brazil-economic-forecast-summary.htm.

[85] *See* Julia E. Sweig, *A New Global Player: Brazil's Far-Flung Agenda*, FOREIGN AFFAIRS (Nov/Dec 2010), http://www.foreignaffairs.com/articles/66868/julia-e-sweig/a-new-global-player (last visited Apr. 10, 2017).

[86] *See* Yilmaz Akyuz, The Rationale For Multilateral Lending; A Critical Assessment 20 (July 5, 2004) (unpublished manuscript), http://www.new-rules.org/storage/documents/ffd/akyuz04.pdf (last visited Sept. 1, 2017).

[87] *See* Article V, Section 3(a) of the Articles of Agreement provides: The Fund shall adopt policies on the use of its general resources, including policies on stand-by or similar arrangements, and may adopt special policies for special balance of payments problems, that will assist members to solve their balance of payments problems in a manner consistent with the provisions of this Agreement and that will establish adequate safeguards for the temporary use of the general resources of the Fund. IMF ARTICLES OF AGREEMENT (last visited Apr. 11, 2017), http://www.imf.org/external/pubs/ft/aa/pdf/aa.pdf. The nature of the conditions have predominantly centered on restricting government spending and foreign borrowing, regulating currency to limit inflation, and in strengthening banking supervision. *See id.*; John W. Head, *Law and Policy in International Finance Institutions: The Changing Role of Law in the IMF and the Multilateral Development Banks*, 17 KAN. J.L. & PUB. POL'Y 194, 214–18 (2007–2008) (discussing the legal aspects of IMF conditionality).

poor countries wanting loans from the IMF and World Bank include privatization-related conditions.[88]

For example, when Bangladesh received a large credit from the World Bank in 2005, of the fifty-three conditions added to the loan, eighteen required that Bangladesh (where over 50 percent of the population lives below the poverty line) privatize its banks, electricity, and tele-communications sectors.[89] Despite these conditions ultimately making matters worse within poorer countries, the average amount of conditions imposed on low income countries rose from forty-eight per loan to sixty-seven per loan between 2002 and 2005.[90]

The World Bank has also been known to impose trade liberalization conditions on poor countries.[91] Rwanda was conditioned to join the East African Trade Agreement, practically stripping its right to freely contract for its exports.[92] Bangladesh was required to remove any quantitative restrictions it had imposed on sugar imports.[93] Luckily,

---

[88] *See* EURODAD, WORLD BANK AND IMF CONDITIONALITY: A DEVELOPMENT INJUSTICE 12 (2006),
http://www.eurodad.org/uploadedfiles/whats_new/reports/eurodad_world_bank_and_i mf_conditionality_report.pdf; *see also Privatization and the World Bank*, THE WHIRLED BANK GROUP (last visited Apr. 11, 2017),
http://www.whirledbank.org/development/private.html (questioning the effectiveness of privatization conditions imposed by the IMF and World Bank, and providing examples of privatization conditions in Argentina, India, and Mexico).
[89] *See id.*; Shahzad Uddin & Trevor Hopper, *Accounting for Privatisation in Bangladesh: Testing World Bank Claims*, SCRIBD (last visited Nov. 13, 2013),
http://www.scribd.com/doc/21894315/Accounting-for-Privatisation-in-Bangladesh-Testing-World-Bank-Claims.
[90] *See id.* at 9.
[91] *See id.* at 12; JUBILEE U.S.A., *Are IMF and World Bank Economic Policy Conditions Undermining the Impact of Debt Cancellation?* (2008),
http://www.jubileeusa.org/fileadmin/user_upload/Resources/Policy_Archive/208briefnot econditionality.pdf ("Some of the most egregious policies force countries applying for debt relief to adhere to strict IMF fiscal and monetary targets, privatize key industries, liberalize their markets, and remove subsidies for sensitive commodities like gasoline and cooking oil.").
[92] *See* EURODAD, *supra* note 89, at 15.
[93] *See id.*; *Bangladesh: Trade Policy and Integration*, THE WORLD BANK (last visited Apr. 11, 2017),
http://web.worldbank.org/WBSITE/EXTERNAL/COUNTRIES/SOUTHASIAEXT/EXTSA

such trade conditions only constitute 3 percent of all World Bank conditions to low-income countries.[94]

In essence, the purpose of the World Bank and IMF in giving loans to poorer countries is to assist those countries in raising their economy while helping to end the cycle of poverty. However, the World Bank has been known to impose "Micro-Management" type conditions, which ultimately prevents much needed aid from reaching those in need of assistance.[95] Uganda, where 37.7 percent of the country lives in poverty, was required to "review and approve its school sports policy for tertiary schools," before it could access its World Bank financing in 2005.[96] As a condition to receiving their financing, The Republic of Mali, where 10 percent of children die as infants, was forced to move its government offices to a new location.[97]

The discord between loan conditionality and development objectives is rooted in the IMF's and World Bank's governance structure that permits dominant shareholders to utilize conditionality as a means of furthering their own global economic and political agendas.[98] Actions by the IMF and World Bank give credence to the growing belief that the major, global institutions "systematically act in the interest of creditors

---

RREGTOPINTECO-
TRA/0,,contentMDK:20592516~menuPK:579454~pagePK:34004173~piPK:34003707~theSit ePK:579448,00.html.

[94] *See* EURODAD, *supra* note 89, at 15.

[95] *See id.* at 11; KENYA NATIONAL ASSEMBLY OFFICIAL REPORT 871 (May 3, 2006) ("The impression that has been created is that...econom[ies] [are] being managed by the IMF and the World Bank. The impression is that all these prices are as a result of micro-management by the IMF and the World Bank.").

[96] *See id.* at 11.

[97] *See id.*

[98] *See* STIGLITZ, *supra* Chapter 1, note 2, at 19 (showing how sometimes conditionality was even counterproductive, either because the policies were not well suited to the country or because the way they were imposed engendered hostility to the reform process); *see contra id.* at 52 (stating that "sometimes money has gone to governments with good policies in place-but not necessarily because the IMF recommended these policies."). Stiglitz also continues the argument that loan conditionalities shifted the debate inside the country in ways that led to better policies. *See id.*

and of rich elite ... in preference to that of workers, peasants, and other poor people."[99]

---

[99] GILBERT RIST, THE HISTORY OF DEVELOPMENT: FROM WESTERN ORIGINS TO GLOBAL FAITH 140–41 (2d ed. 2006) (explaining that people in industrial countries began to complain that Third World demands were being ignored, causing the underdevelopment of the Global South). While transnational corporations were getting rich, countries of the South were being exploited for their resources. *Id.*

3

CASE STUDIES

T o continue the analysis in the preceding chapter of the global impact of Neoliberalism, this chapter presents case studies on Argentina, Africa, and Asia, and investigates how the neoliberal approach of the IMF and World Bank has impacted those countries.[1]

Argentina

Argentina provides a context to examine the economic and human impact of IMF lending over the course of nearly half a century. Prior to World War I, Argentina was viewed by the public and investors as a land of opportunity.[2] Argentina was a resource-rich nation and therefore attracted both European and American investors.[3] The Great Depression negatively affected Argentina due to its reliance on exporting capital.

Argentina initially appealed to the IMF for assistance in 1958 in hopes of receiving an infusion of capital to address its rampant inflation and a resulting balance of payment crisis.[4] The early successes associated

---

[1] *See infra* Chapter III.D.

[2] *See* KRUGMAN, *supra* note 21, at 38–40.

[3] *See id.*

[4] *See* KRUGMAN, *supra* note 21, at 51; Argentina's lower profile rescue came via the World Bank, which enabled a capital injection of $12 billion to support the nation's banks. *See id.* Subsequently, the Fund conditionally provided capital in the amount of 75 million

with the loans were mitigated by an emerging discontent within the labor force stemming from a decrease in real wages, a rise in inflation, and a decline in the country's gross domestic product.[5]

Argentina's internal political problems led to a problematic relationship with the IMF until, in 1965, President Arturo Illia terminated Argentina's relationship with the IMF, rejecting all of the IMF's conditions and attempting to deal unilaterally with the $2.5 billion Argentina owed to international creditors.[6] By failing to comply with the IMF's policies, Illia eroded international confidence in the Argentinean economy. This was reflected in the severe decline of international loans to the country over the next three-year period, and thus, Illia suffered the same fate as his Argentinean predecessors.[7]

In a 1967 coup d'état, Colonel Juan Ongania seized presidential power and agreed to implement an IMF stabilization program, which mandated the same fiscal deficit and inflation goals that had relegated Argentina to a constant state of political and economic turmoil since

---

and a further 254 million dollars, which was derived from public and private U.S. agencies. *See id.*

[5] *See* Margaret Conklin & Daphne Davidson, *The I.M.F. and Economic and Social Human Rights: A Case Study of Argentina, 1958-1985*, 8 HUM. RTS. Q. 231–32 (1986) (explaining that in 1959 real wages, decreased by twenty-six percent from the previous year, inflation rose to 111%, and GDP declined by eight percent). As the working class became increasingly dissatisfied, Argentina had a record number of employee strikes. *Id.* Even after the Fund negotiated similar stand-by arrangements for 1959 and 1960, the atmosphere within Argentina was not positive because the allocation of the funds wasconditioned upon the attainment of strict deficit reduction goals that were reliant upon "large dismissals of employees, limitation on wage increases, and a reduction in public works." *Id.*

[6] *See Argentina: Going It Alone*, TIME (Apr. 30, 1965), http://www.time.com/time/magazine/article/0,9171,898668,00.html (last visited Apr. 11, 2017) (explaining how Illia had attacked the IMF during his campaign for president, calling it an economic intruder and recommending that Argentina break relations with the Fund).

[7] *See* Conklin & Davidson, *supra* note 104, at 234. International loans to Argentina fell drastically, from 361 million in 1962, to 99 million in 1963 and 6 million in 1964. *See* Conklin & Davidson, *supra* note 104, at 234. The military overthrew Illia in June 1966. *See id.*

1958.[8] However, in 1969 the IMF proclaimed a successful stabilization effort in Argentina based on an increase in its gross domestic product and reduction in the inflation rate.[9] These economic indicators seemingly validated the IMF's policies, but failed to resonate in the hearts of the Argentinean people who had been forced to adapt and survive on real wages that had fallen 11 percent in 1968.[10]

Starting in 1970, and continuing throughout the next three decades, the citizens of Argentina galvanized together against the IMF and fought for political changes as the IMF remained resolute in its conviction that the "shock therapy" approach was the right path for Argentina to attain progress and prosperity.[11] After a further decline in real wages in 1978, only ten percent of the population had the economic means to purchase the government's shopping basket of basic goods and services.[12] After struggling with massive inflation rates and a costly war that ended in 1982, Argentina appealed to the IMF for aid.[13] The startling figures

---

[8] *See* Conklin & Davidson, *supra* note 104 at 235. Conditions in 1967 and 1968 including the devaluation of the peso, limits on fiscal deficit (increased utility charges for public services, restraints on government spending, and higher internal taxes), and wage controls (wage freezes until 1968). *See id.*

[9] *See* KRUGMAN, *supra* note 21, at 41 (comparing Mexico and Argentina's positive reaction to capital inflows when inflation dropped to nearly zero and GDP increased by 25% in three years).

[10] *See* Conklin & Daphne Davidson, *supra* note 104, at 236.

[11] *See* Kim Reisman, *World Bank and the IMF: At the Forefront of World Transformation*, 60 FORDHAM L. REV. 349, 390 (1991–1992) (explaining that shock therapy is a means used by the IMF and World Bank to establish a market economy in countries by inflicting the attendant hardships for as short a time as possible in contrast to an evolutionary or gradual approach).

[12] *See* Conklin & Davidson, *supra* note 104, at 245–52 (explaining that in the years of 1976 to 1978, public sector employees had their wages decreased by 53%, so that the government could comply with the Fund's fiscal deficit targets). The Fund's demand to reduce government expenditures translated to massive cuts and layoffs of public sector employees who were already "paid among the lowest in Argentina." *See id.* Although the deficit declined, the citizens were confronted with the reality that the cost of gas, telephone, water, rail fares, electricity, postal charges, and metro fare had increased an average of 405 percent. Conklin & Davidson, *supra* note 104, at 245–52.

[13] *See id.* at 239; *I.M.F. Loan to Argentina*, N.Y. TIMES (Jan. 25, 1983) http://www.nytimes.com/1983/01/25/business/imf-loan-to-argentina.html?mcubz=0 (explaining that in early 1983, the IMF approved a $2 billion loan, including $1.5 billion SDR, to improve the collapsing economy).

taken in the 1980's illuminate a blatant disregard by the IMF to balance the human cost of economic stabilization with the benefits of attaining arbitrary economic indicator targets.[14] The problems of inflation and economic stagnation in the 1980's culminated in the hyperinflation that occurred in 1989.[15]

In 1991, Argentina instituted a Convertibility Plan designed to stabilize the economy through drastic measures, including fixing the peso to the U.S. dollar.[16] The Convertibility Plan and structural reforms led to stabilization, and the IMF believed that the six percent average GDP growth through 1997 was a sign of the success of these measures.[17] However, the appreciation of the currency placed exports and domestic producers at a disadvantage because payments became more difficult to make. The rise in prices ultimately led to a balance of payment issue. In 1995, the payment issue was coupled with government public relations problems with the IMF, and eventually resulted in the decline of the stock market.[18] Additionally, laws influenced by the IMF condi-

---

[14] *See* Conklin & Davidson, *supra* note 104, at 245–52 (explaining that a study in 1985 estimated that one third of employed workers failed to earn sufficient wages so as to be able to feed a family of four); Milt Freudenheim, Henry Ginger, & Richard Levine, *A Heartfelt Cry From Alfonsin On Debt Crisis*, N.Y. TIMES, (Mar. 24, 1985) , at 42 (explaining the plight of President Raul Alfonsin in 1985). Alfonsin's presidency followed eight years of military rule. *Id.* During his presidency, inflation began eating away at the standard of living to a point where Alfonsin had to balance the IMF's demands for austerity measures with the demands by Argentinean wage-earners for pay increases. *Id.*

[15] *See* INT'L MONETARY FUND INDEP. EVALUATION OFFICE, THE ROLE OF THE IMF IN ARGENTINA, 1991-2002 (July 2003), http://www.imf.org/external/np/ieo/2003/arg/070403.pdf [hereinafter The Role of the IMF].

[16] *Id.* (defining the Convertibility Plan). It was centered around a currency board-like arrangement in which the peso was fixed at par with the dollar and autonomous money creation by the central bank was severely constrained. *Id.* "[I]t also included a broader agenda of market–oriented structural reforms to promote efficiency and productivity." *Id.*

[17] *Id.*

[18] *See* Juan Carlos Linares, *After the Argentine Crisis: Can the IMF Prevent Corruption in its Lending? A Model Approach*, 5 RICH. J. GLOBAL L. & BUS. 13, 19 (2005) (explaining how Argentina was forced to renegotiate its IMF loan, leading to the stock market decline).

tions, along with changes to the social security system, ultimately sparked massive "anti-IMF riots" in 1998.[19]

Later, in mid-2001, the lack of access to capital markets caused an increased capital flight that, in turn, resulted in Argentina's financial collapse later that year.[20] Once again, as had happened repeatedly before 1991, Argentina was unable to meet IMF conditions and the IMF suspended disbursements.[21] The Convertibility Plan was widely criticized for failing to account for Argentina's internal conditions. Linking the currency with the U.S. dollar forced Argentina to "align its monetary policy with that of the United States, despite cyclical differences between the two countries."[22]

The IMF's negative involvement in Argentina culminated in January 2002, when the government of Argentina defaulted on $141 billion in public sector debt; this was "the largest sovereign default" of a state in history.[23] The catalyst behind Argentina's default and economic collapse has been "attributed to the country's excessive adherence to International Monetary Fund advice."[24] Argentina's 2009 statement that it does not need the IMF's financial help seems tenuous at best, as ear-

---

[19] Id. at 20 (describing the situation in Argentina around the time prior to the anti-IMF riots). The IMF's bailouts were seen as protecting the affluent at the expense of the poor. Id. The austerity programs installed to pay for the IMF loans were said to be absorbed by the poor instead of the wealthy. Id.

[20] See The ROLE OF THE IMF, supra note 114.

[21] See id. (explaining how this led to the abandonment of the Convertibility Plan and, by the end of 2002, the economy had contracted by twenty percent since 1998).

[22] See id.; see Linares, supra note 117, at 23 (explaining other factors that contributed to the economic collapse, including decline in capital flows, institutional and political factors unique to Argentina, external shocks, failures in the banking system, and systemic corruption that was inherent in Argentina's politics and economy).

[23] See Linares, supra note 117, at 18–9 (explaining the steps taken by the IMF and Argentina, starting in 1991 to its default in December 2001). Argentina's relationship with the IMF from 1990's through 2000 was marked by a series of renegotiations to loan agreements and requests for financial assistance. See id. Although Argentina never really complied with any of the IMF conditions, the IMF was unwilling to abandon its work there. See id. Meanwhile, Argentinean citizens and businesses found themselves marred in government tax increases and spending reductions. See id.

[24] See Jo Marie Griesgraber & Oscar Ugarteche, The IMF Today and Tomorrow: Some Civil Society Perspectives, 12 GLOBAL GOVERNANCE 351 (2006).

lier that same year Argentina demanded IMF loans without conditions.[25] It has been stated that "the success story of the Argentine stabilization program can be best told by international creditors as...they have been paid punctually and...could hardly be happier regarding the success of International Monetary Fund recommendations."[26]

In August 2016 the Executive Board of the IMF met to consider the Managing Director's report on Argentina's economic progress.[27] The report was made possible when the Argentinian government finally allowed IMF economists to enter the country following the institution's "censure" of Argentina for failing to pay its debts. [28] This was the IMF's first Article IV visit in nearly a decade.[29]

Sub-Saharan Africa

The BWI have been responsible for the most numerous set of policies ever enacted by Sub-Saharan African countries.[30] Either directly, or as

---

[25] *See* Walter Brandimarte, *Argentina Demands IMF Lend Without Conditions*, REUTERS (Apr. 24, 2009), http://www.reuters.com/article/idUSN2445415920090424; Sujata Rao & Carolyn Cohn, *Argentina Says Does Not Need Aid From IMF*, REUTERS (Sept. 5, 2009, 2:30 PM), http://www.reuters.com/article/idUSTRE58429020090905.

[26] Conklin & Davidson, *supra* note 104, at 259–60 (explaining how the Fund consistently went against the poor and working-class Argentineans). The Argentine government, faced with many hardships, had poor bargaining power against the Fund. *See id.*

[27] *See* Raphael Anspach, *Statement by the IMF Executive Board on Argentina*, INTERNATIONAL MONETARY FUNDS (Aug. 31, 2016), https://www.imf.org/en/News/Articles/2016/08/31/PR16389-Statement-by-the-IMF-Executive-Board-on-Argentina (stating the Executive Board of the IMF was made aware of Argentina's "authorities' extraordinary efforts and important progress made in strengthening the accuracy of Argentina's statistics. A revised series for GDP has been produced that is broadly in line with international standards, and a new CPI series has been launched that aims to address the inaccuracies in the previous index").

[28] *See IMF returns to Argentina*, DEUTSCHE WELLE (Sept. 20, 2016), http://www.dw.com/en/imf-returns-to-argentina/a-19563153 (stating the "International Monetary Fund is set to arrive in Buenos Aires . . . for the first time in a decade. It ends years of hostility to the lender from previous governments.").

[29] *See id.* (stating the IMF's impediment was due to "[t]he late President Nestor Kirchner barr[ing] the IMF from carrying out the annual reviews of member states' economic health in 2006.").

[30] *See* AFRICAN DEVELOPMENT BANK, AFRICAN DEVELOPMENT REPORT 55 (2006) (listing the IMF and World Bank conditionality's in Sub–Saharan Africa as of 1999 as: Cameroon 92;

a consequence, the World Bank and IMF are responsible for policies that led to significant changes in African economies.[31] Even with the implementation of these policies, Sub-Saharan Africa is still one of the poorest regions in the world and so unlikely to meet the Sustainable Development Goals[32] by the established date.[33]

During the 1950's and 1960's, the World Bank concentrated on the development of physical infrastructure.[34] Through the 1970's, the Bank's

---

Djibouti 134; Gambia 121; Ghana 80; Guinea 125; Madagascar 137; Mali 105; Mozambique 74; Rwanda 135; Senegal 165; Tanzania 150; Uganda 74; and Zambia 87).

[31] *See* REGIONAL SURVEYS OF THE WORLD: AFRICA SOUTH OF THE SAHARA 2004 20 (Katherine Murison ed., 33d ed. 2003) (explaining how the IMF and World Bank have pushed pressured Sub–Saharan African countries to large scale economic reforms). In 1998, thirty-five African countries began economic reform programs or borrowed from the IMF to support economic reform programs. *Id.* A 1981 World Bank study proposed four economic policy changes including: (1) the correction of overruled exchange rates; (2) the improvement of price incentives for exports and agriculture; (3) the protection of industry in a more uniform and less direct way; and (4) the reduction of direct governmental controls. *Id.; see* GÉRARD ROLAND, PRIVATIZATION: SUCCESSES AND FAILURES 44 (2008) (explaining that most of these policies concentrated on the goals of privatizing and stabilizing the economies). The hope was for economic growth and financial development results to follow. *Id.* Many of the newly private companies, instead of contributing to the growth of the economy, actually worsened the population's situation by laying workers off. *Id.* In Zambia for example, two large mines were sold to a bidder who agreed not to dismiss any of the workers. *Id.* However, after title was transferred, three thousand of the seven thousand workers were dismissed, and subsequently, the new owner went out of business causing the remaining four thousand workers to lose their jobs. *Id.*

[32] *See Sustainable Development Goals*, UNITED NATIONS DEV. PROGRAMME (last visited Apr. 10, 2017), http://www.un.org/sustainabledevelopment/sustainable-development-goals/ (laying out the 17 Sustainable Development Goals, which include: ending poverty and hunger; universal education; gender equality; child health; maternal health; combating HIV, AIDS and other diseases; environmental sustainability; global partnership among other). *See also supra* Chapter I, note 21 and accompanying text.

[33] *See* SAUL BERNARD COHEN, GEOPOLITICS: THE GEOGRAPHY OF INTERNATIONAL RELATIONS 31 (Rowman & Littlefield Publishers, 2009) (explaining that the average per capita income in Sub-Saharan Africa is $2,500, and 30% of the working poor earn less than one dollar per day); JEFFREY SACHS, COMMON WEALTH: ECONOMICS FOR A CROWDED PLANET 31 (2008) for a discussion on the history of Sub-Saharan Africa's poverty and lack of development in comparison with the United States and United Kingdom; *see also* ROB BOWDEN, AFRICA SOUTH OF THE SAHARA 10 (Heinemann, 2008) (stating that the World Bank has said that twenty–two of the twenty–five poorest countries in the world are in Sub-Saharan Africa, Burundi being the poorest of the world, with an average annual income per person of $640).

[34] *See* PHILIP W. JONES, EDUCATION, POVERTY AND THE WORLD BANK 11 (Sense Publishers, 2006).

lending shifted and concentrated more on social areas like education, water access, poverty reduction, and income distribution.[35] However, as the 1980s approached, most economic leaders were conservative and favored economic liberalization and maintaining governments at the edge of the economic markets.[36] In 1963, the IMF started lending to Sub-Saharan Africa; however, the number of loans granted to the area was relatively small until the 1970's.[37]

The World Bank, influenced by conservative economists, adopted this approach, which was reflected in the policies it pushed Sub-Saharan African countries to employ.[38] Lending during the 1980s became conditioned on economic policy reforms, and by the end of the decade, there was practically no difference between the World Bank's and IMF's conditionality terms.[39] Some countries that received aid in Sub-Saharan Africa were at times undeserving, due to the political and economic turmoil present within.[40]

---

[35] *See* JOHN WILLIAMSON, THE IMPACT OF THE BRETTON WOODS INSTITUTIONS ON THE PROSPECTS FOR DEVELOPMENT, *in* SOUTH AFRICA AND THE WORLD ECONOMY IN THE 1990'S 178, 179 (The Brookings Inst., Pauline H. Baker et al eds., 1993). From his first speech to the Board of Governors, McNamara spoke of directing Bank lending toward improving the living conditions of individual poor people, and proposed expanding education lending to emphasize advanced technical training as well as fundamental literacy. *Id.; see* MARTHA FINNEMORE, NATIONAL INTERESTS IN INTERNATIONAL SOCIETY 107 (1996); RONALD G. RIDKER, THE WORLD BANK'S ROLE IN HUMAN RESOURCE DEVELOPMENT IN SUB-SAHARAN AFRICA: EDUCATION, TRAINING, AND TECHNICAL ASSISTANCE 42 (The World Bank, 1994) (explaining that these were the goals of the World Bank's president at the time, Robert McNamara).

[36] *See* WILLIAMSON, *supra* note 134.

[37] *See* ROBERT S. BROWNE, THE IMF IN AFRICA: A CASE OF INAPPROPRIATE TECHNOLOGY, *in* 3 THE POLITICAL MORALITY OF THE INTERNATIONAL MONETARY FUND: ETHICS AND FOREIGN POLICY (Robert J. Myers ed., 1987).

[38] *See* WILLIAMSON, *supra* note 134.

[39] *See* IDA'S PARTNERSHIP FOR POVERTY REDUCTION: AN INDEPENDENT EVALUATION OF FISCAL YEARS 1994–2000 77 (2002); Howard Stein, *Structural Adjustment*, *in* THE ELGAR COMPANION TO DEVELOPMENT STUDIES 599 (David A. Clark ed., 2006).

[40] *See* KENDALL W. STILES, NEGOTIATING DEBT: THE IMF LENDING PROCESS 69, 75 (1991) (describing the IMF's loan to Zaire). Zaire's Chief of State, Mobuto Sese Seko, began talks with the IMF in 1976, and a forty-seven million dollar one-year stand-by loan was approved. *Id.* The loan called for a forty-two percent devaluation to align Zaire with the SDR; a twenty percent ceiling on wage increases; a cut of government expenditures in-

Both the World Bank and the IMF still subject African countries to dozens of conditions in order to receive loans. The conditions are mainly focused on lowering government expenses on social issues and diverting them towards market liberalization in order to cover forgone government revenues from lowering export barriers.

These corrective reforms were seen as necessary by many due to the crisis experienced by the African countries in the early 1980s. The goal for countries participating in the SAP was to achieve economic stability in the short-term and further growth and development in the long-term. However, many argue that these adjustments did not promote long-term development.[41]

---

volving foreign exchange; a twenty-two percent limit on domestic credit expansion during 1976; and a renegotiation of external public debt. *Id.* Zaire became ineligible for further assistance in 1977 because it failed to meet conditions of the loan and repay debts. *Id.* at 72, 76. Zaire provided the IMF with disjointed, uncoordinated, and confused financial information that "tried the patience of the IMF to its limit." *Id.* It also became clear to Zaire's creditors that Zaire had not intent to implement the IMF reforms. *Id.* In 1978, at the urging of Zaire's creditors, the IMF sent officials to replace local Zairian financial leadership, and other stand-by arrangement of $155 million was given in 1979. *Id.* at 69, 76. Zaire's political aristocracy frustrated the efforts of the IMF team, and thus the loans were cancelled by 1983. *Id.* at 70, 74. The willingness of the IMF to keep returning to Zaire with loans was deemed "startling" in the context that Zaire's performance indicated its unwillingness to meet the terms of its loans. *Id.* at 79, 83.

[41] *See* SALIWE M. KAWEWE, POLITICS AND ECONOMICS OF AFRICA, VOL. 5 43 (Olufemi Wusu ed., 2007) (stating that if governments fail to meet the measures imposed, any loans that may have been promised to them are withheld or canceled); THE POLITICS AND POLICIES OF SUB–SAHARAN AFRICA 73 (Robert A. Dibie ed., 2001) (stating that "the conditions attached to World Bank and IMF structural adjustment program . . . effectively transferred sovereignty from the African State to Washington") [hereinafter THE POLITICS AND POLICIES]; *see id.* (stating that the World Bank and IMF force governments to reduce spending on basic human needs and necessities like the elimination of subsidies for food prices, and reduction or social welfare and programs, including health and education); VINCENT B. KHAPOYA, THE AFRICAN EXPERIENCE: AN INTRODUCTION 182 (1998) (explaining how the IMF has required governments from Sub-Saharan Africa to reduce budget deficits by making cuts on expenditures on public programs); *see Africa: Hazardous to Health*, UNIVERSITY OF PENNSYLVANIA - AFRICAN STUDIES CENTER 1, 5 (Apr. 18, 2002), https://www.africa.upenn.edu/Urgent_Action/apic-041802.html (indicating that the loans were intended to reduce deficits and assist in closing the gap in trade between important and exports. However, they evolved into a set of required economic policies implemented by the World Bank and IMF); *See* KAWEWE, *supra*, at 44 (noting Zimbabwe as an example where the elimination of price controls on manufactured goods, retrenchment of

The results of these conditions are lower salaries, impoverishment for Africans, and cheaper raw materials for multinational companies. Sub-Saharan African countries have accumulated increasingly high debt allowances, whereby interest outlay payments to financial institutions exceed income from loans, which result in harmful net outflows of cash.[42]

The IMF's and World Bank's structural reforms have proven to be inefficient and detrimental to the people in Sub-Saharan Africa.[43] After adhering to the IMF's and World Bank's policies and mandated structural adjustments, residents of Sub-Saharan African countries have not experienced any long-term improvement in their living conditions.[44] But with the voting power in the IMF of all Sub-Saharan African countries together accounting for only about a fourth of that allocated to the

---

works, devaluation of currency, and privatization of government industries resulted in a sharp shrinkage of income opportunities for the urban middle class and the working class).

[42] *See generally id.* The elimination of price controls simultaneously marginalizing the poor further, especially women and children. *Id.*; RICHARD PEET, UNHOLY TRINITY: THE IMF WORLD BANK AND WTO 141 (2007) (stating that during the 1980's when most African countries came under World Bank and IMF tutelage, per–capita income decreased by twenty five percent in most of Sub–Saharan Africa). In addition, the removal of food and agricultural subsidies caused prices to rise and created increased food scarcity. *Id.* Since between one–fourth and one–third of the population of Sub–Saharan Africa is malnourished, the vulnerability of African populations to the spread of diseases and other health problems, has increased. *Id.* This, coupled with the closing of numerous hospitals and the understaffing of the ones remaining, has only added to the problems rampant within Sub–Saharan Africa. *Id.*; *see* THE ENCYCLOPEDIA OF AFRICAN HISTORY: VOLUME 1 338 (Kevin Shillington ed., 2004).

[43] *See* REGIONAL SURVEYS OF THE WORLD: AFRICA SOUTH OF THE SAHARA 2004 119 (Katherine Murison ed., 33d ed. 2003) (explaining the case of Burkina Faso which highlights the inefficiencies of the policies) [hereinafter REGIONAL SURVEYS OF THE WORLD]. Since the 1970's there has been a history of fiscal deficit in Burkina Faso which has been mainly attributable to the economy's low taxable capacity. *Id.* In 1993 the IMF accorded an Enhanced Structural Adjustment Facility to Burkina Faso. *Id.* Under the terms of the accord the primary objective was to reduce the fiscal deficit, which was at 4.6% of GDP. *Id.* However, by 1994, instead of decreasing, the deficit had actually increased to 5.1% of GDP. *Id.* By 1999, the deficit was still four percent of GDP. *See id.*

[44] *See* Andrew Conteh, *Sub–Saharan Africa in the Post Cold War Era, in* THE POLITICS AND POLICIES OF SUB–SAHARAN AFRICA 73–6 (Robert A. Dibie ed., 2001).

United States alone, their voice is not likely to bring about any major reform.[45]

Specifically, Senegal received its first IMF loan in 1984.[46] Since its independence from France in 1960, Senegal has had a strong democratic system and is one of the most stable countries in Africa.[47] Even though Senegal's annual per capita growth was only 0.6 from 1987 to 2015, lower than all other fast-growing countries, Senegal is considered one of the most stable economies in Africa.[48]

In the late 1980s and early 1990s the IMF and World Bank's recommendations led to drastic social sector spending cuts and numerous layoffs.[49] Under the structural adjustment program, the government

---

[45]*See* International Monetary Fund, Annual Report 2009 47, http://www.imf.org/external/pubs/ft/ar/2009/eng/index.htm (last visited Oct. 21, 2013) (showing that the aggregated voting power for all Sub-Saharan countries is 4.36 percent, while the Unites States alone holds 16.77 percent); Maurilo Portugal, *Improving IMF Governance and Increasing the Influence of Developing Countries,* IMF DECISION-MAKING, IN REFORMING THE GOVERNANCE OF THE IMF AND THE WORLD BANK 75, 83 (Ariel Buira ed., 2006) (explaining Sub-Saharan Africa's voting power); *see also* MARCUS POWER, RETHINKING DEVELOPMENT AND GEOGRAPHIES 84 (2003) (explaining that similarly, in the World Bank, the G8 states hold ten times the voting power of all Sub-Saharan countries together). The G-8 states hold forty percent of the voting power in the World Bank, while Sub-Saharan Africa holds just over four percent. *Id.*

[46] *See* Kingston, Kato Gogo, *The Impacts of the World Bank and IMF Structural Adjustment Programmes on Africa: The Case Study of Cote D'Ivoire, Senegal, Uganda, and Zimbabwe (2011),* SACHA JOURNAL OF POLICY AND STRATEGIC STUDIES.

[47] *See Senegal GDP growth reaches 6.5% for first time in 12 years: IMF,* REUTERS, http://economictimes.indiatimes.com/articleshow/51371073.cms?utm_source=contentofin terest&utm_medium=text&utm_campaign=cppst (indicating that Senegal's GDP growth reached 6.5% for first time in 12 years).

[48] *The Impacts of the World Bank and IMF Structural Adjustment Programmes on Africa: The Case Study of Cote D'Ivoire, Senegal, Uganda, and Zimbabwe,* https://www.researchgate.net/publication/233868994_The_Impacts_of_the_World_Bank_and_IMF_Structural_Adjustment_Programmes_on_Africa_The_Case_Study_of_Cote_D %27Ivoire_Senegal_Uganda_and_Zimbabwe. ("Political Economists argue that, Africa's underdevelopment has largely resulted from the ways in which African states have been created and political authority shaped through interactions with the developed countries in the context of global economic and political systems.").

[49] *See* Alieu Darboe, *Senegal: 1974- present,* INTERNATIONAL CENTER ON NONVIOLENT CONFLICT (2010). In 1992, 40 percent of the population was classified as hungry. In 1994, the devaluation of the CFA Franc led to riots and strikes due to the fact that people could not afford any imported items, such as medicines. *See id.*

also had to cut education expenditures; unemployment had risen over twenty percent in 1996.[50] In the late 1990s the IMF Board commissioned an independent evaluation of its work in Africa.[51] Contrary to the goals of these institutions, export expansion and foreign investment did not increase growth or reduce poverty and debt. Scholars and International NGOs that have studied Africa's development question whether these policies imposed by the IMF and World Bank have actually helped.[52] Some critics of the Brentwood Institutions strongly state that these policies did the opposite of their intended plan.[53]

Currently, Senegal participates in the IMF's, non-financial instrument, Policy Support Instrument (PSI) under the Poverty Reduction and Growth Trust. The PSI provides monitoring and support to low-income countries that "do not want-or need- fund financial assistance but seek to consolidate their economic performance."[54] The PSI also helps countries design economic programs that are effective and that will demonstrate the strength of the member's economic policies. However, scholars in the area have indicated that these policy conditions, known as conditionalities, which have been implemented to try to resolve the

---

[50] *See* Alieu Darboe, *Senegal: 1974- present*, INTERNATIONAL CENTER ON NONVIOLENT CONFLICT (2010) (explaining that "unemployment in Dakar rose from 25% in 1991 to 44% in 1996"); *see* UNITED NATIONS, WORLD ECONOMIC SITUATIONS AND PROSPECTS 2009 21 (2009) (explaining how the decrease in demand for exports, lower commodity prices, and decline in investments in the Sub–Saharan African region resulting from the crisis, will affect Sub–Saharan African countries' economic development).

[51] *See* Ngaire Woods, *Governance matters: the IMF and Sub-Sahara Africa*, Oxford University Press (2008).

[52] *The Impacts of the World Bank and IMF Structural Adjustment Programmes on Africa: The Case Study of Cote D'Ivoire, Senegal, Uganda, and Zimbabwe*,
https://www.researchgate.net/publication/233868994_The_Impacts_of_the_World_Bank_ and_IMF_Structural_Adjustment_Programmes_on_Africa_The_Case_Study_of_Cote_D %27Ivoire_Senegal_Uganda_and_Zimbabwe.

[53] *See* ASAD ISMI, IMPOVERISHING A CONTINENT: THE WORLD BANK AND THE IMF IN AFRICA (2004) ("[C]ontrary to World Bank dogma, export expansion and rising foreign investment in Africa have not increased growth or reduced debt and poverty–in fact, as seen below, they have had exactly the opposite effect.").

[54] *See* Arne Bucker and Ronald Labonte, *The financial crisis and global health: the International Monetary Fund's (IMF) policy response*, HEALTH PROMOTION INTERNATIONAL (2012).

IMF policy limits implemented in many countries, have not been care-
fully planned out and have had a negative impact on these countries.[55]

The new development strategy was implemented in early 2014, as a
response to the low growth performance.[56] This strategy focuses on
creating productive employment opportunities to sustain a higher
growth rate, unlocking the agricultural productivity and becoming a
competitive market participant. This posed a significant challenge for
Senegal in terms of job creation for the younger generation, as well as
for curbing the country's high poverty rate. The IMF required African
countries to reduce state support and did not invest in health, education and infrastructure before making these changes. This caused the
economic development in the African countries to stall even more.[57]

---

[55] *See World Bank and IMF Conditionality: a development injustice*, EURODAD (June 2006)
http://www.eurodad.org/uploadedfiles/whats_new/reports/eurodad_world_bank_and_i
mf_conditionality_report.pdf ("Current IMF and World Bank conditionality is fundamentally flawed. Not only are these institutions imposing far too many conditions on
poor countries, but many of the conditions are at best wholly inappropriate, and at worst,
harmful to the poor people and undermine national ownership."); *see also* Akanksha A.
Marphatia, THE ADVERSE EFFECTS OF INTERNATIONAL MONETARY FUND PRO-
GRAMS ON THE HEALTH AND EDUCATION WORKFORCE, *Debates on International
Agencies: Critiques of the IMF*,
http://citeseerx.ist.psu.edu/viewdoc/download?doi=10.1.1.878.4318&rep=rep1&type=pdf
(explaining that the policy conditions set out by the IMF have imposed low wage ceilings
and "indirectly influenced governments in setting the limitations" that ultimately affect
the countries social sector); Ismi, *supra* note 152.
[56] *See The Impacts of the World Bank and IMF Structural Adjustment Programmes on Africa:
The Case Study of Cote D'Ivoire, Senegal, Uganda, and Zimbabwe*,
https://www.researchgate.net/publication/233868994_The_Impacts_of_the_World_Bank_
and_IMF_Structural_Adjustment_Programmes_on_Africa_The_Case_Study_of_Cote_D
%27Ivoire_Senegal_Uganda_and_Zimbabwe. Prior to participating in this plan, Senegal
was admitted to the Heavily Indebted Poor Countries (HIPC Initiative) in 2010. "By that
admission, Senegal agreed to receive US$800 million, or US$450 million in Net Present
Value (NPV) in debt relief over a 10-year period. The IMF and the World Bank were to
contribute US$45 million and US$116 million to Senegal, respectively over a 9-year period. Sadly, the relief stated above only accounted for just 17% of the country's debt burden. Thus, had little or no meaningful impact in a country where at least 65 % of the
population live on the equivalent of less than one dollar a day." *See id.*
[57] *See* Anup ShahThis, *Structural Adjustment—a Major Cause of Poverty*, GLOBAL ISSUES-
SOCIAL, POLITICAL, ECONOMIC AND ENVIRONMENTAL ISSUES THAT AFFECT US ALL (Mar.
24, 2013), http://www.globalissues.org/article/3/structural-adjustment-a-major-cause-of-
poverty ("African countries require essential investments in health, education and infra-

The IMF Executive Board completed its first review under the PSI for Senegal and indicated that economic growth was projected at five percent for 2015 and almost six percent in 2016—numbers that were lower than what was actually achieved.[58] In 2015, Senegal reported an economic growth of over six percent for the first time in more than 10 years.[59]

On April 12, 2017, the IMF staff completed its fourth PSI review visit, in which it indicated that the "macroeconomic performance remained solid in 2016, with GDP growth above six percent for the second consecutive year. Inflation remains low, owing to low international oil prices and an elevated supply of products on the market. The external current account deficit improved due to higher exports and workers' remittances." [60]

Asian Crisis

The Asian financial crisis destroyed "the conventional wisdom that East Asia's economies would prosper indefinitely."[61] While few schol-

---

structure before they can compete internationally. The World Bank and IMF instead required countries to reduce state support and protection for social and economic sectors. They insisted on pushing weak African economies into markets where they were unable to compete with the might of the international private sector. These policies further undermined the economic development of African countries.").

[58] *See* IMF, Senegal: Seventh Review Under the Policy Support Instrument and Request for Modification of Assessment Criteria - Staff Report; and Press Release, Country Report No. 14/177, 1 (July 2014) ("Senegal's new growth strategy offers a good diagnostic and a vision for Senegal," but could still face problems due to "insufficient progress in reform implementation combined with strong expenditure pressures.").

[59] *See Senegal: Economic growth climbs to 6.5%, first time in more than a decade*, AFRICA NEWS (Mar. 13, 2016) http://www.africanews.com/2016/03/13/senegal-economic-growth-climbs-to-65-percent-first-time-in-more-than-a-decade// (indicating that the growth is a consequence of Senegal's two-year-old economic plan and agricultural sector).

[60] *See* Lucie Mboto Fouda, *IMF Staff Completes the Fourth PSI Review Visit to Senegal*, INTERNATIONAL MONETARY FUND (Apr. 12, 2017), https://www.imf.org/en/News/Articles/2017/04/12/pr17129-senegal-imf-staff-completes-the-fourth-psi-review-visit (reporting the IMF staff team's preliminary findings after their Senegal visit).

[61] Peter A. Coclanis & Tilak Doshi, *Globalization in Southeast Asia*, 570 ANNALS, July 2000, at 49, 56-7 (explaining that few would have predicted the crisis because leading up to 1995 because per capita growth in Singapore, Indonesia, Malaysia, and Thailand was

ars predicted such crisis,[62] it exposed the flaws of IMF loan conditionality and consequences of global financial liberalization[63] The "[f]inancial liberalization from the 1980's had major ramifications in the region as savings supplemented the already high domestic savings rates in the region to further accelerate the rate of capital accumulation."[64]

Although there are at least four competing explanations for how the Asian financial crisis began,[65] it officially started in July 1997 in Thailand, after the Thai government began to float its currency, the Thai baht.[66] At that time, "the growth of bank and nonbank credit to the

---

much greater in comparison to that of South Asia and Latin America); JEFFREY D. SACHS & WING THYE WOO, UNDERSTANDING THE ASIAN FINANCIAL CRISIS, THE ASIAN FINANCIAL CRISIS: LESSONS FOR A RESILIENT ASIA 13 (Wing Thye Woo, Jeffrey D. Sachs, & Klaus Schwab, eds.) ("The World Bank and International Monetary Fund…are now divided on the causes of the crisis, and on what the policy advice should have been given."). *But see* Paul Krugman, *The Myth of Asia's Miracle,* 73 FOREIGN AFF. 62, 64 (1994) (explaining, before the Asian Crisis began, that the rapid Asian growth that occurred at the beginning of the 1990's was not a model that the West should follow, and that future growth would be limited).

[62] *See* JOMO K.S., GROWTH AFTER THE ASIAN CRISIS: WHAT REMAINS OF THE EAST ASIAN MODEL? 2 (Mar. 2001), http://www.unctad.org/en/docs/pogdsmdpbg24d10.en.pdf; *see also* STIGLITZ, *supra* Chapter I note 2, at 6 (arguing how decisions concerning necessary reforms in global institutional arrangements must be made not by a self-selected group such as the G-7, G-8, G-10, G-20, or G-24, but should be made by all the countries of the world).

[63] *See id.*

[64] MANUEL F. MONTES, THE CURRENCY CRISIS IN SOUTHEAST ASIA 1 (2000) (listing four competing explanations of the Asian financial crisis). The four explanations are: the entry of low cost producers into the international export markets; macroeconomic weakness in all economies; undisciplined banking; or the shear differences between all of the different countries' economies. *Id.; see* Laurent L. Jacque, *The Asian Financial Crisis: Lessons from Thailand,* 23 FLETCHER F. WORLD AFF. 87 (1999) ("[T]he Asian crisis primarily originated in the private sector. It is a crisis of flawed resource allocation abetted by misguided government policies and unfortunately corrected by Western style policies often ill-adapted to the idiosyncrasies of Asian capitalism.").

[65] *See* SACHS & WOO, *supra* note 160, at 13 (explaining the confusion among experts as to how the financial crisis occurred even after analysts had been praising Asian economies up until the unexpected collapse in July 1997).

[66] *See* MORRIS GOLDSTEIN, THE ASIAN FINANCIAL CRISIS: CAUSES, CURES, AND SYSTEMIC IMPLICATIONS 7 (1998); Helen Hughes, *Crony Capitalism and the East Asian Currency Financial 'Crises',* POLICY (Spring 1999) http://www.cis.org.au/POLICY/Spr99/polspr99–1.htm (last visited Nov. 23, 2017) (explaining that most East Asian banks did not adopt the proper accountability and transparency measures necessary to police loaning practices, thus a high proportion of those loans were non-performing).

private sector exceeded…the already rapid growth of real GDP…[and] exposure to the property sector accounted for roughly twenty-five to forty percent of total bank loans in Thailand, Indonesia, Malaysia, and Singapore, and more than that in Hong Kong."[67] With an overextension and concentration of credit, countries became vulnerable to shifts in cyclical and credit conditions.

By the end of 1997, Indonesia, Malaysia, South Korea, Thailand, and the Philippines' stock markets had lost more than sixty percent of their value.[68] "[T]he Indonesian rupiah was down more than 80 percent against the dollar, and the currencies of Thailand, Malaysia, and Philippines all fell by 30–50 percent … [w]ithin months of the baht flotation, the stock markets of all four saw losses of sixty percent or more in dollar terms."[69] Most surprisingly affected by the crisis was South Korea, because at the onset it was the most rapidly growing country in the region and the eleventh biggest economy in the world. Yet after the crisis hit, South Korea lost its credibility as it became known that its banks lacked "commercial orientation" and had made too many risky loans.[70]

At the center of some of the criticism before the crisis was the IMF, whose inappropriate advice "led to overly tight macroeconomic poli-

---

[67] *Id.* at 8–9 (explaining that falling property prices and rising shares of nonperforming bank loans were a consequence of the ASEAN–4 economies being vulnerable to the shifts in credit and cyclical conditions). In an effort to minimize borrowing costs, too much of those countries' borrowing consisted of short maturities and/or foreign currency; an ultimately risky strategy as it contributed to currency mismatches. *Id.; see Overview, the Association of Southeast Asian Nations*, ASEAN (last visited Nov. 23, 2017), http://www.asean.org/asean/about-asean/overview (providing an overview of ASEAN).
[68] *See* Coclanis & Doshi, *supra* note 160, at 59 (describing these events as the "Asian flu" or "bahtulism"); *see also* Jomo K.S., *supra* note 161, at 12 (discussing how the Republic of Korea's currency, the won, collapsed, and as a result, the Hong Kong dollar was directly attacked).
[69] Coclanis & Doshi, *supra* note 160, at 59; *see* Jomo K.S., *supra* note 161, at 12.
[70] *See* John W. Head, *Global Implications of the Asian Financial Crisis: Banking, Economic Integration, and Crisis Management in the New Century*, 25 WM. MITCHELL L. REV. 939, 945–46 (1999) (explaining how South Korea's financial difficulties basically forced it to accept an IMF bailout package in December 1997). At the time, South Korea's twenty-one billion-dollar IMF loan was the largest the IMF ever made. *Id.*

cies and badly designed and badly handled restructuring programs."[71] Besides persuading Thailand into devaluation, the IMF was alleged to have pressured Indonesia to devalue the rupiah, which also led to devaluation in the Philippines and South Korea, and the needless "debasing" of the Taiwan dollar.[72]

The World Bank was not immune from criticism either, as just four years prior to the crisis it argued that Indonesia, Thailand, and Malaysia were the preferred economic models for other developing countries to emulate.[73] Both the IMF and World Bank encouraged Asian countries to adopt a strategy known as "fast-track capitalism" which ended up putting countries in high-yield, yet high-risk sectors; this ultimately led to the crisis.[74]

After the crisis broke, the IMF attempted to come to the countries' rescue by instituting "programmes and conditionalities, as well as policies favored by the international … financial communities and others affected."[75] Its three-point strategy was aimed toward financing, macroe-

---

[71] SACHS & WOO, supra note 160, at 14; see Hughes, supra note 165 (criticizing the IMF for funding countries that had balance of payment difficulties). This led to a moral hazard where private lenders and developing country borrowers relied upon the IMF for perpetual credit. See id. The author goes on to criticize the World Bank for giving loans to countries "that had no intention of following prudent economic policies." See id.

[72] See Editorial, The IMF Crisis, WALL ST. J., Apr. 15, 1998, at A22 (describing the IMF's mishandling of Asia's economy). "The IMF tripped this crisis by urging the Thais to devalue, then, promoted contagion by urging everyone else to do likewise." Id.

[73] See Jomo, supra note 161, at 1–2 (explaining The East Asian Miracle study conducted by the World Bank in 1993 that the World Bank sought to distance itself from). The study concluded, in contrast to the majority of case-studies such as those in Latin America and Africa, that structural adjustment programs were working in East Asia. See id.

[74] See Jomo, supra note 161, at 23–4; see John W. Head, Lessons from the Asian Financial Crisis: The Role of the IMF and the United States, 7 KAN. J.L. & PUB. POL'Y 70, 71–74 (1998) (detailing the IMF's bailout package broken down by country and dollar amounts); PETER G. ZHANG, IMF AND THE ASIAN FINANCIAL CRISIS 73–4, 78 (1998) (explaining, for example, how at the peak of the crisis, the IMF loaned South Korea fifty-eight billion dollars on December 4, 1997). The IMF's immediate response was to help Korea, Indonesia, and Thailand design programs of structural economic reforms to win investors' confidence. Id. The loans did not curb the financial crisis, because, for example, the South Korean won ended up falling to 1,745 wons for every U.S. dollar on January 23, 1998. Id.

[75] IMF Staff, Recovery from the Asian Crisis and the Role of the IMF, INT'L MONETARY FUND (June 2000), http://www.imf.org/external/np/exr/ib/2000/062300.htm#III (listing the three

conomic policy, and structural reform within Indonesia, South Korea, and Thailand.[76] The IMF's programs "urged bank closures, government spending cuts and higher interest rates in the wake of the crisis."[77] In the end, the IMF's aid failed as its programs were contradictory in consequence and exacerbated the impact of the crisis in countless aspects.[78]

In a review of its handling of the Asian Crisis of 1997 to 1998, the IMF recognized that it needed to improve the infrastructure of the international financial system.[79] The IMF Managing Director, Dominique Strauss-Kahn, echoed this realization by stating that "the Fund has ad-

---

components of the IMF's Asian crisis rescue plan). Although the IMF initially put in thirty-five billion dollars of support for Indonesia, Korea, and Thailand to be distributed equally, eventually, Indonesia got more money, in 1998 and 1999. *Id.* The macroeconomic policies affected were monetary and fiscal policies. *Id.* Money was tightened to stop the collapse of each country's exchange rate and, especially in Thailand, fiscal policy was tightened to diminish deficit increases. *Id.* Finally, structural reforms were taken to address corporate and financial sector weaknesses. *Id.*

[76] *See* Jomo, *supra* note 161, at 23–4.

[77] *See id.; see* Editorial, *Dousing the IMF Fires*, WALL ST. J., Oct. 8, 1998, at A18. "Before you pour liquid on a raging fire…make sure it doesn't smell like gasoline…the IMF doesn't look like much of a fireman." *Id.* In March 1997, IMF Managing Director Michel Camdessus encouraged Thailand to devalue its currency, but as the Asian crisis proves, this was a huge mistake. *Id.* Then, the IMF gave eighteen billion to Thailand, forty-three billion to Indonesia, and fifty-seven billion to South Korea. *Id.* Those loans, coupled with loans to Russia and Brazil, totaled $171 billion from the beginning of the Asian Crisis through 1998 as the crisis continued. *Id.* In 1997, Camdessus predicted that the crisis would not be prolonged. *See id.* His prediction looked foolish for the IMF to have stood behind at the time. *Id. But see Letters to the Editor: A Gross Distortion of IMF's Policies*, WALL ST. J., May 29, 1998, at A15 (discussing IMF External Relations Department Director Shailendra Anjaria's contention that the IMF did not force Thailand to devalue its currency).

[78] *See The IMF's Response to the Asian Crisis*, INT'L MONETARY FUND (last visited Nov. 23, 2017), http://www.imf.org/External/np/exr/facts/asia.htm (explaining the six major areas where the IMF should be strengthened: (1) more effective surveillance over countries' economic practices and policies; (2) financial sector reform; (3) ensuring orderly and properly sequenced integration of international financial markets; (4) pro-moting regional surveillance; (5) promoting good governance and fighting corruption; and (6) more effective structures for orderly debt workouts).

[79] *See* Neil Watkins, *The London G-20 Summit: The Global New Deal We Need*, JUBILEE USA NETWORK 1, 3 (Mar. 3, 2009), http://www.jubileeusa.org/fileadmin/user_upload/Resources/G20/Briefing_note_G20_London_Summit.pdf (quoting Managing Director of the IMF, Dominique Strauss-Kahn).

vocated fiscal stimulus to restore global growth ... [t]here is now a broad consensus on this."[80] The lessons of the Asian Crisis have not manifested themselves within the framework of the policy advice that has been directed toward countries battling the current economic crisis.[81]

The nature of the conditions attached to the loans symbolizes the IMF's unresponsiveness and systematic inability to avoid the historic cyclical pattern of providing loans to those without the sufficient financial and economic systems set in place to provide for timely repayment--the cost of which has been nothing less than a country's sovereignty.[82]

---

[80] *See id.* at 4 (discussing the recent history of the IMF in its loans to Serbia, El Salvador, Latvia, and Hungary). Serbia was told that anything less than a tight fiscal stance would jeopardize the credibility of the program in the eyes of foreign investors and the Serbian public. *Id.* A loan to El Salvador in January of 2009 advocated the attainment of economic growth through the administering of tax increases and diminishing gas and transport subsidies. *Id.* In funding a December 2008 loan to Latvia, the lending was contingent upon reduction in many government related expenditures as well as the incorporation of a value added tax. *Id.* The implementing of stringent fiscal deficit and inflation targets were also a critical component of the loan to Hungary in November 2008. *See id.* The IMFs polices toward developing countries differ from its policies toward developed countries. Watkins, *supra* note 178, at 4.

[81] *See* PAUL BLUSTEIN, THE CHASTENING: INSIDE THE CRISIS THAT ROCKED THE GLOBAL FINANCIAL SYSTEM AND HUMBLED THE IMF 382 (Pub.Affairs) (2003) (suggesting that instead of attaching conditions, loans should only go to countries that pre-qualify by adhering to certain banking standards); *see also infra* Chapter IV.

[82] *See* STIGLITZ, *supra* Chapter I note 2, at 84 (proposing countercyclical lending to countries in distress in order to stabilize the suffering economies); *see id.* (stating how lending at higher rates in a cyclical manner will infringe upon the economic recovery of the nation). The policies pushed by the international financial institutions are now seen as having contributed to the lack in confidence in these institutions and the loan conditionalities they imposed. *See id. See Ten years on How Asia shrugged off its economic crisis*, THE ECONOMIST (Nov. 9, 2017), http://www.economist.com/node/9432495 (demonstrating the level of recovery experienced ten years after the 1997 Asian crisis, the author breaks down the efforts of each crisis-affected country); Takehiko Nakao, *What the 1997 Asian financial crisis has taught us*, TODAY (Nov. 7, 2017), http://www.todayonline.com/world/asia/what-1997-asian-financial-crisis-has-taught-us (explaining how the region has recovered twenty years after it was affected by the crisis). In Thailand, the Bank of the Thailand imposed regulations to control the inflow of capital. *Ten years on How Asia shrugged off its economic crisis, supra.* The author states how most of the private sector's short-term debt took the form of trade credits versus loans. *Id.* Additionally, the author states how the process of consolidation in the banking sector, which has been under way since 2004, and regulatory standards and bank lending practices

Bangladesh

Bangladesh's history provides a prime example of how international financial agencies, like the World Bank, extend support accompanied with numerous conditions in order to accelerate the privatization process in developing countries, only to realize that said process may not produce the expected results. [83] Before the Bangladesh Liberation War,[84] Bangladesh—formerly known as East Pakistan (FN) – was well

---

have noticeably improved the country. *Id.* In Indonesia, new investment laws were set to make conducting business within the country easier. *Id.* The implementation of post-crisis economic and financial reforms in South Korea has allowed the country's financial sector to become one of the Asian region's strongest country combined with greater openness through better regulation. *Id.* Through these practices, South Korea's foreign reserves were able to rise from "US$8.9bn to US$243bn at the end of March 2007." *Id.* After "major restricting in the financial sector and the build-up of foreign-exchange reserves sufficient enough to sustain more than eight months of retained imports" Malaysia has transformed into a more financially stable country. *Id.* Hong Kong, one of the worst countries hit in the crisis, did not recover until 2005. *Id.* As a result of the fast-growing mainland Chinese economy, increased trade with China led to a big increase in Hong Kong's re-export trade and caused massive expansion for Hong Kong's financial services sector. *Id.* The author points out how the crisis-affected countries were able to recover by "adopting more flexible exchange rates, strengthening financial sector regulation and governance, and implemented structural reforms." Nakao, *supra.* Additionally, the author points out how the adoption of more judicious approaches to "capital account liberalism" has allowed these once crisis-affected countries to grow by 6.8 percent yearly in the past two decades and rely more on domestic demand twenty years later. *See id.*

[83] *See* A. K. M. Masudul Haque, *Privatisation in Bangladesh: A Case of Placing the Cart before the Horse,* 6 U.W. Sydney L. Rev. 123, 125 (2002) (explaining that the World Bank believes that the economies of developing countries are not efficient due to public enterprises not operating at expected profits and that subjecting the public sector to the discipline of privatization will be more efficient). *But see* John E. Kwoka, *Public vs. Private Ownership and Economic Performance: Evidence from the U.S. Electric Power Industry* 1, 2 (Jan. 1995), https://www.hks.harvard.edu/hepg/Papers/Kwoka_Ownership_0295.pdf (stating that empirical evidence provides that the hypothesis indicating that public enterprises are less efficient than private owned has a weak support system).

[84] *See* Mark Dummett, *Bangladesh War: The Article That Changed History,* BBC NEWS (Dec. 16, 2011), http://www.bbc.com/news/world-asia-16207201 (indicating that "[t]he conflict was sparked by elections, which were won by an East Pakistani party, the Awami League, which wanted greater autonomy for the region. [T]he political parties and the military argued over the formation of a new government [and] [t]he situation started to become violent. The Awami League launched a campaign of civil disobedience...."); *Liberation War of Bangladesh,* Bangladesh News (Mar. 23, 2008), http://www.independent-bangladesh.com/history/liberation-war-of-bangladesh.html (explaining that the war did

recognized for the size of its population, political representation, and economy.[85] After the war, the independent nation sought foreign aid to help forge a new nation under the rule of presidents and ministers with different agendas.[86] Within a month of the war's conclusion, India loaned Bangladesh $232 million, with the majority of it available for immediate disbursement.[87] But an agreement between Bangladesh and the World Bank was not finalized until several months later.[88]

---

not occur overnight, but has been brewing since 1947 due to political and economic deprivation of East Pakistan in comparison to West Pakistan).

[85] *See* Haque, *supra* note 182, at 166.

[86] *See* James Heitzman and Robert Worden, *Bangladesh: A Country Study*, COUNTRYSTUDIES.US (1989), http://countrystudies.us/bangladesh/55.htm (stating that the World Bank created an alliance composed of twenty-six foreign governments and financial institutions known as the Bangladesh Aid Group; designed to assist the nation in its development); *see also Bangabandhu Sheikh Mujibur*, BANGLAPEDIA (Dec. 10, 2015), http://en.banglapedia.org/index.php?title=Rahman,_Bangabandhu_Sheikh_Mujibur (explaining Mujibur Rahman as the first president of the newly liberated nation in 1971); *Bangladesh Reports Death of President Ziaur Rahman*, THE NEW YORK TIMES (May 30, 1981), http://www.nytimes.com/1981/05/30/world/bangladesh-reports-death-of-president-ziaur-rahman.html (stating that General Ziaur Rahman seized power of the nation for six years after the assassination of Mujibur Rahman); *See* Haque, *supra* note 182, at 133–34 (indicating that the General "opted for a much greater role for the private sector…to increase the boundaries of private investment while cutting the size of public enterprises [subjecting] [i]ndustries reserved to the public sector…to joint participation of public and private enterprises."); Rosanna Kim, *Bangladeshis Bring Down Ershad Regime, 1987-1990*, GLOBAL NONVIOLENT ACTION DATABASE (Nov. 18, 2012), http://nvdatabase.swarthmore.edu/content/bangladeshis-bring-down-ershad-regime-1987-1990 (explaining that General Hussain Muhammed Ershad, like General Ziaur, seized power in 1986 under martial law and assumed presidency until 1990); *Bangladesh War of Independence*, New World Encyclopedia, http://www.newworldencyclopedia.org/entry/Bangladesh_War_of_Independence (indicating that the separation of East and West Pakistan resulted from the thesis that Muslims and Hindus could not live in harmony, eventually causing an uprising when the West attempted to impose an official language on the East). The war lasted nine months, after which Bangladesh surfaced as an independent nation from West Pakistan, now known as Pakistan. *Id.*

[87] *See* Heitzman & Worden, *supra* note 185.

[88] *See id.; see also International Bank for Reconstruction and Development (IBRD) Board of Governors resolution; no. 274: Membership of Bangladesh*, THE WORLD BANK (June 13, 1972), http://documents.worldbank.org/curated/en/923761468014360579/International-Bank-for-Reconstruction-and-Development-IBRD-Board-of-Governors-resolution-no-274-Membership-of-Bangladesh (showing a membership contract between Bangladesh and the World Bank in 1972 for aid, highlighting conditions—such as gaining membership to the IMF—that must be met prior admission).

The delay in the World Bank's aid to the government was in part due to the outstanding debt that Pakistan, before the Bangladeshi split, incurred prior 1971, amounting to nearly $3 billion.[89] Although Bangladesh made it clear that the debt issue was to be resolved between them and Pakistan, the World Bank refused to accept this notion and no aid was provided until the government accepted liability for past debts on projects commenced within its borders.[90]

Bangladesh was under no obligation to assume Pakistan's liability, absent a direct agreement with the creditors, even though a substantial portion of the territory was divided.[91] This "illustrates the power and leverage that can be exerted by external creditors, including international financial institutions, and in particular the World Bank, in the process of negotiations on debt issues, and explains why Bangladesh had ultimately to [sic] accept a part of the external debt liability."[92]

Post Liberation War, the government was left to manage hundreds of businesses left behind by entrepreneurs and industrialists fleeing the war, announcing its decision to nationalize the major industries and banking organizations as it moves toward a socialistic ideology.[93] The idea slowly withered away under the rule of Mujibur Rahman Khan (Mujib) as the government began to allow private investments with imposed ceilings after the declaration of Investment Policy.[94]

There is a strong implication that the occurrence of these events began shortly after Bangladesh was approved as a member of the World Bank

---

[89] See JUST FAALAND, AID AND INFLUENCE: THE CASE OF BANGLADESH 128 (Nurul Islam et al. eds., 1981) (explaining that Pakistan argued that Bangladesh is liable for the debt for improvements within its border).

[90] See id. at 128–29 (stating that the Bangladesh eventually yielded due to pressures from creditors and prisoners being held in India after the war).

[91] See id. at 129.

[92] Id.

[93] See Haque, supra note 182, at 129–30 (creating thirty-eight new public corporations within the first year in comparison to the twenty that existed before the war).

[94] See id. at 130–31.

in June 1972.[95] This same agreement, aside from its conditions, contained a prerequisite that the government become a member of the IMF, opening multiple avenues for the World Bank to impose its ideals of privatization.[96]

Inferring that foreign-aid organizations induced the implementation of privatizing resources in the country is not far-fetched, however, because within the first year and a half of Liberation, the country implemented its First Five Year Plan (1973—1978) that clearly laid out a framework leading to nationalization.[97]

Although there were limitations on private investments, due to certain activities in the trade industry, there was a surplus of funds in private hands by 1974, and these same private investors alongside foreign-aid investors, pressured the government to increase the private investment ceiling four-fold.[98] However, the development of the nationalization

---

[95] *See International Bank for Reconstruction and Development (IBRD) Board of Governors resolution; no. 274: Membership of Bangladesh*, THE WORLD BANK (June 13, 1972), http://documents.worldbank.org/curated/en/923761468014360579/International-Bank-for-Reconstruction-and-Development-IBRD-Board-of-Governors-resolution-no-274-Membership-of-Bangladesh.

[96] *See id.*

[97] *See* Nurul Islam, *The First Five Year Plan 1973—78*, PLANNING COMMISSION 1, 1 (Nov. 1973) http://www.plancomm.gov.bd/wp-content/uploads/2016/04/Part-14.pdf ("Our nationalism…only enjoins on us that we take upon ourselves the responsibility of bringing about the cultural, social, and economic development of the Bangalees."); *see also* Fakrul Ahsan, *Development Planning In Bangladesh: Historical Perspective*, ECONOMIC RELATIONS DIVISION 1, 9 http://erd.portal.gov.bd/sites/default/files/files/erd.portal.gov.bd/page/2f97258a_6f25_479 a_8545_a498c65783f2/Development%20Planning%20Process_Fakrul%20Ahsan.pdf (showing the actual annual average growth is not as high as the first five year plan until the fourth five year plan); Muhammad Fazlul Hassan Yusuf, *Nationalisation of Industries in Bangladesh: Political and Administrative Perspectives*, UNIVERSITY OF TASMANIA 1, 2 (Dec. 1980), http://eprints.utas.edu.au/21768/1/whole_YusufMuhammadFazlulHassan1982_thesis.pdf ("The fundamental principles of State policy as set forth in the Consti- tution, the primary objectives of the State as outlined in the FFYP [First Five Year Plan] and political guidance and directives were the source-base of formulation and implementation of government policies.").

[98] *See* Haque, *supra* note 182, at 131 (illustrating that the World Bank recommended that the ceiling be removed or raised). However, the new investment policy increased private investments, three times the amount the World Bank suggested it be increased to. *See id.*

policy and the limitations on private investment quickly changed once the military seized power from the Awami League[99] in 1975.[100]

Martial law was lifted under the rule of General Ziaur Rahman,[101] ultimately shifting the government's vision to privatizing investments in the country.[102] "As a result compensation provisions were liberalized, generous incentive packages were introduced for the private sector, scope of private industrial investment was expanded and sales to private investors of smaller enterprises abandoned earlier by non-locals and taken over by the government were expedited."[103]

A World Bank sponsored review of Bangladesh and other case studies have shown that industry productivity depends on the efficiency of management and not ownership.[104] Private enterprises were closing

---

[99] *See* Heitzman & Worden, *supra* note 185 ("The Awami League traces its descent from the party of Sheikh Mujibur Rahman, and in the late 1980s it continued to advocate many of the socialist policies of the early 1970s.").

[100] Muhammad Fazlul Hassan Yusuf, *Nationalisation of Industries in Bangladesh: Political and Administrative Perspectives*, UNIVERSITY OF TASMANIA 1, 4 (Dec. 1980), http://eprints.utas.edu.au/21768/1/whole_YusufMuhammadFazlulHassan1982_thesis.pdf .

[101] *See* Heitzman & Worden, *supra* note 183 (describing the General as a ruthless opponent but nonetheless a charismatic political figure that was declared the nation's most prominent leader since independence); *see also* Kasturi Rangan, *Bangladesh Leader is Shot and Killed in a Coup Attempt*, THE NEW YORK TIMES (May 31, 1981) http://www.nytimes.com/1981/05/31/world/bangladesh-leader-is-shot-and-killed-in-a-coup-attempt.html?mcubz=0 (explaining that martial law was lifted once General Ziaur's government was overwhelmingly supported).

[102] *See* Nasim Ahmed, *The Initiation and Promotion of the Privatization Policy of State Owned Enterprises in Bangladesh: Political- Economic Factors and the Role of Major Policy Actors*, ASIAN AFFAIRS 18, 23 (Oct.—Dec. 2008), http://citeseerx.ist.psu.edu/viewdoc/download?doi=10.1.1.471.8285&rep=rep1&type=pdf (stating that the General "perceived a further deterioration of macro politico-economic condition," therefore "abandoning nationalization...would strengthen the political base and would enhance stability of the military government."); Clare E. Humphrey, *Privatization in Bangladesh*, USAID 1, 60 (May 1987), http://pdf.usaid.gov/pdf_docs/PNABD867.pdf (indicating that the government extended all support to the private sector believing it to be the most efficient and dynamic).

[103] Muhammad Fazlul Hassan Yusuf, *Nationalisation of Industries in Bangladesh: Political and Administrative Perspectives*, UNIVERSITY OF TASMANIA 1, 4 (Dec. 1980), http://eprints.utas.edu.au/21768/1/whole_YusufMuhammadFazlulHassan1982_thesis.pdf

[104] *See* A *See* Haque, *supra* note 182, at 152 (explaining that it is extremely difficult to measure a countries performance based solely on the change of ownership).

down and others experienced problems. This forced the World Bank to come to a similar conclusion that privatization produces mixed results.[105] A survey in 1993 conducted by Bangladesh revealed that of the 498 privatized enterprises surveyed, less than half were operational, 133 were closed down, and 141 were untraceable.[106]

Nonetheless, even though this case study raises questions on the effectiveness of privatization, a politically weakened country depending on foreign aid to bolster its economy only enhances the authority of international lending agencies in implementing their privatization ideals.[107]

In 2009, Bangladesh began proposals and negotiations with the IMF and World Bank for a loan from its Extended Credit Facilities (ECF) program.[108] After several years of delays and preparations, the loan scheme was concluded in 2015, and the IMF granted Bangladesh a $987-million-dollar loan.[109] The loan came with eleven conditions that needed to be met before Bangladesh could receive the IMF funds.[110]

These conditions, many of which are typically attached to such loan programs, included:

---

[105] *See id.* at 152-53.

[106] *See id.* at 153.

[107] *See* Shahzad Uddin and Trevor Hopper, *Accounting for Privatisation in Bangladesh: Testing World Bank Claims*, RESEARCHGATE 1, 6 (Oct. 2003), http://repository.essex.ac.uk/16709/1/worldbankrep3.doc.pdf (indicating that "[i]nternational lending agencies became a major influence upon government policies.").

[108] *See* Rejaul Karim Byron & Sarwar A Chowhury, *IMF Concludes Loan Scheme*, THE DAILY NEWS STAR (October 23, 2015), http://www.thedailystar.net/business/imf-concludes-loan-scheme-161263.; *see* Campaign Paper, *Conditionality of Receiving $1bn IMF Loan Is Suicidal*, Equity BD Organization (April 24, 2011), http://www.equitybd.net/wp-content/uploads/2015/09/campaign_imf_26042011.pdf.

[109] *See* Byron & Chowhury, *supra* note 207.

[110] Rashed Al Mahmud Titumir, et al., *Bangladesh Economic Update: IMF's Loan and its Implications on Bangladesh Economy*, ECONOMIC POLICY UNIT OF THE UNNAYAN ONNESHAN (Volume 2, No. 2, March 2011) http://www.unnayan.org/documents/Governance%20Capability/meu_Mar_2011.pdf; *see also* ARTICLE 2 (noting that "[i]f this proposed loan of IMF is disbursed, 11 steps will have to be taken by the country as per agreed conditionalities, some of which will not in Bangladesh's interests.").

- pursuing a contractionary monetary policy to control inflationary pressure;
- further liberalization of tariff level;
- moving into a floating exchange rate regime as a more liberal exchange regime;
- placing new value-added tax (VAT) and income tax to achieve revenue targets;
- phasing out bank lending rate ceilings, as part of bringing in greater flexibility in the lending regime;
- raising CNG and furnace oil prices;
- auditing of SCBs accounts for the year 2010.[111]

Pursuing a "contractionary monetary policy" is one of the major conditions set for negotiating the IMF's one-billion-dollar loan.[112] The government has implemented this condition and national banks have already experienced increased interest rates.[113] As the IMF stated, Bangladesh has to follow a tight monetary and fiscal policy to control its inflationary pressure.[114]

Notably, the IMF failed to identify the real cause of Bangladesh's inflation: "The IMF advocated Bangladesh to pursue a tight monetary policy assuming that the country is facing inflation which is demand pull in nature [,] when [in] reality, the inflation in Bangladesh is due to supply shock."[115]

---

[111] *See* Titumir, *supra* note 209 (noting that "[w]ith the implementation of these prescriptions, Bangladesh, like many others, had to swallow all disastrous contracts with multinational companies that paved the way for their plundering natural resources and witnessed the silent erosion of national capabilities.").

[112] *See id.*

[113] *See* Campaign Paper, *supra* note 207; *see also* National Dialogues, *Borrowing From the IMF will Limit Bangladesh Government's Fiscal Flexibility: Remarked CPD*, CENTRE FOR POLICY DIALOGUE (February 13, 2011) http://cpd.org.bd/borrowing-from-the-imf-will-limit-bangladesh-governments-fiscal-flexibility-remarked-cpd/ (highlighting that according to the CPD study done in 2011, the contractionary monetary policy conditionality could ultimately lead to an increase in the interest rate.)

[114] *See* Titumir, *supra* note 209.

[115] *See* Titumir, *supra* note 209.

In Bangladesh, inflation—especially in food prices—continues to tick up due to the shortage of supply of basic food items in the local markets, as well as because of supply shock inflation in the global market.[116] To control supply shock inflation, augmenting the level of production can be an effective step along with other necessary measures. On the other hand, tight monetary policies in demand-pull inflation might create a reverse effect by driving up inflation and increasing the balance of payment pressure.[117] Adopting a tight monetary policy would reduce the availability of credit to the commercial bank. The ultimate effect will be the reduction of credit availability to the people, which would increase interest rates.[118]

Under the IMF's conditions, Bangladesh Bank has recently removed the interest rate ceiling to allow commercial banks to move on the market-based rates. In fact, the Bangladesh Bank has recently raised the Statuary Liquidity Ratio (SLR), Cash Reserve Ratio (CRR), as well as removed the lending interest cap as a major requirement under IMF's one-billion-dollar loan.[119] The removed lending rate caps affect the following sectors: commercial credit, working capital, housing loan and loan to non-bank financial institutions. The effect of such measures might be counterproductive on the overall performance of the macro economy.[120] The higher lending interest rate and the discrimination of charging interest rates among various commercial banks tempered international interest of investment in Bangladesh.[121] In 2009, Bangladesh

---

[116] *Id.; see also* CNN World Columnist, *Riots, Instability Spread As Food Prices Skyrocket,* CNN NEWS (April 14, 2008)
http://www.cnn.com/2008/WORLD/americas/04/14/world.food.crisis/.

[117] *See* Titumir, *supra* note 209.

[118] *See id.; see also* National Dialogues, *Borrowing From the IMF will Limit Bangladesh Government's Fiscal Flexibility: Remarked CPD,* CENTRE FOR POLICY DIALOGUE (February 13, 2011) http://cpd.org.bd/borrowing-from-the-imf-will-limit-bangladesh-governments-fiscal-flexibility-remarked-cpd/ (highlighting that according to the CPD study done in 2011, the contractionary monetary policy conditionality could ultimately lead to an increase in the interest rate.).

[119] *See id.*

[120] *See* Titumir, *supra* note 209.

[121] *See id.*

Bank imposed the maximum limit of interest rates at 13% in an effort to boost investment.[122]

The gross domestic savings as share of GDP dropped from 20.31% in FY 2008 to 18.99% in FY 2010.[123] Concurrently, a decline was observed both in public and private sector savings.[124] The reduction in volume of investments is expected to put pressure on the national output that may reduce employment rates in the country, which might in turn reduce the overall income level.[125] The shock in the domestic market will ultimately increase inflation. Thus, the combined effect of reduction in income level and an increasing inflationary pressure is likely to cause a drastic reduction in savings.[126]

Removing the lending interest rate ceiling will increase the lending interest rate, which will have an adverse impact on investment.[127] Without corrective measures, the existing low-investment phenomenon in Bangladesh is likely to worsen.[128] Investment levels are positively related to GDP growth.[129] Thus the reduction of investment would cause a negative impact on the level of production, which will in turn increase the supply shortage of output. Additionally, the purchasing

---

[122] *See id.*

[123] *See id.*

[124] "Private sector savings in GDP also dropped slightly from 18.96 percent to 17.72 percent from FY 2008 to 2010 respectively, which was mainly due to higher consumption expenditure. [And] the ratio of *public* savings declined from 1.35 percent in FY 2008 to 1.27 percent in FY 2010." *See id.*

[125] *See id.*

[126] *See* Titumir, *supra* note 209.

[127] *See id.*

[128] *See id.; see also* National Dialogues, *Borrowing From the IMF will Limit Bangladesh Government's Fiscal Flexibility: Remarked CPD*, CENTRE FOR POLICY DIALOGUE (February 13, 2011) http://cpd.org.bd/borrowing-from-the-imf-will-limit-bangladesh-governments-fiscal-flexibility-remarked-cpd/.

[129] *See* Titumir, *supra* note 209; World Bank's Lead Economist, Mr. Sanjay Kathuria, observed that "investment should exceed savings in a country like Bangladesh. . . . For this the government has to ensure a transparent and regulatory environment to attract foreign direct investment." *See* National Dialogues, *Borrowing From the IMF will Limit Bangladesh Government's Fiscal Flexibility: Remarked CPD*, CENTRE FOR POLICY DIALOGUE (February 13, 2011) http://cpd.org.bd/borrowing-from-the-imf-will-limit-bangladesh-governments-fiscal-flexibility-remarked-cpd/.

power of the people will continue to decrease as the food inflation continues to rise.

The dual effect of reducing the national output and savings with an increased interest rate might cause unemployment to further increase the general inflation rate. This would create an unrealistic burden on the government to achieve the projected GDP growth rate of 10.7% in 2017.[130]

Further liberalization of the trade regime by reducing the tariff rate and removing trade barriers are also major requirements for Bangladesh to receive the IMF's loan under the ECF program.[131] Generally, the removal of both import and export duty creates pressure on both sides. Bangladesh is an import-dependent country, and because the benefit of removing the tariff depends on the economic strength and nature of the particular country, this trade liberalization would reduce "per unit import cost, while the quantity of import is likely to increase, which would eventually amplify the overall import volume."[132] Accordingly, the total import cost would outweigh the total export earnings. This would ultimately increase the trade deficit.[133]

Additionally, liberalization of the tariff level might prevent local industries from growing, as it would lessen the government's authority to regulate market mechanisms already in place.[134] If both the export and import duties are fully liberalized, the goods and services of other countries will enter the local market quite easily. This would force local industries to face sure competition in the form of highly subsidized products from India, China, the United States, and Malaysia.

---

[130] *See* Titumir, *supra* note 209.

[131] *See id.*

[132] *See id.*

[133] *See id.*

[134] *See* Titumir, *supra* note 209 (underscoring that "[t]he cotton and weaving industries in Bangladesh were in a very strong position as these had a huge demand in the local market as a backward linkage industry of the Ready Made Garments (RMG). Currently, the Bangladeshi cotton and weaving industries are on the brink of collapse as the Indian cotton is replacing the local industry.").

Consequently, if mechanisms to protect the local industries are not in place, unemployment would continue to rise in Bangladesh with the introduction of outsourced products. Among the local industries that would face the threat of extinction due to trade liberalization are sugar, cotton and the woven industries.[135] Trade liberalization would pave the way for Indian sugar to dominate the local market.[136]

Currency depreciation has occurred in Bangladesh over the years as a result of adopting flexible exchange rates gradually.[137] Still, the IMF is lobbying Bangladesh to change its current managed floating exchange rate system and to a clean floating exchange rate system, in which the exchange rate of taka would be determined by the interaction of demand and supply of currency in the foreign exchange market.

Adopting a floating exchange rate system does not necessarily mean that the currency will be depreciated. Currency might appreciate or depreciate, depending on the nature of the country's trade balance. Consequently, the floating exchange rate would lead to currency depreciation in an import-based country like Bangladesh.[138] IMF's conditionality for the one-billion-dollar loan might exert serious pressure over GDP growth in Bangladesh.[139]

As an import-oriented country, Bangladesh would most likely face hardship as its import costs rise from its currency depreciation, which eventually hikes price levels in the domestic market.[140] Bangladesh earns a sizable amount of foreign exchange by exporting some specific

---

[135] *See id.*

[136] *See id.*

[137] "During the FY 2004 – 05, the exchange rate was 61.39 and in FY 2005 – 06 it was 67.39 with a 9.25 percent depreciation of BDT against USD during the same period of time. In FY 2007-08, the exchange rate was 68.60 appreciating 0.62 percent of BDT against USD compared to the previous year as a result of global recession. During FY2008-09, the exchange rate was 68.80 and in FY 2009- 10 it was 69.19 meaning a BDT depreciation of 0.29 percent from FY2007-8 to FY 2008-09. The depreciation continued from the FY2009-10 to FY 2010-11 by 0.56 percent and 2.66 percent respectively." *See id.*

[138] *See* Titumir, *supra* note 209.

[139] *See id.*

[140] *See id.*

products, such as readymade garments, leather, shrimp, jute, medicine, and recently from its ship industry.[141] If the currency continues to depreciate, the earnings from the export sector would expand, prompting domestic exporters to export more. Depreciation also might create supply shock in the domestic market, causing prices to rise.[142]

Although the Bangladeshi government and parliament publicly announced plans to pass the proposed tax reforms since 2011,[143] it was not until June 2017 that Bangladesh was able to do so.[144] In its yearly Budget, released June 1, 2017, Bangladesh declared corporate income tax cuts and the introduction of the new value-added tax law (VAT) to be collected at any stage.[145] An increase in VAT will be collected from poor and marginalized people during any purchases of daily goods.[146] The new tax plan cuts corporate taxes for the readymade garment industry from 20% to 15%, or to 14% for those companies with internationally recognized green building certifications.[147]

---

[141] *See id.; see also* National Dialogues, *Borrowing From the IMF will Limit Bangladesh Government's Fiscal Flexibility: Remarked CPD*, CENTRE FOR POLICY DIALOGUE (February 13, 2011) http://cpd.org.bd/borrowing-from-the-imf-will-limit-bangladesh-governments-fiscal-flexibility-remarked-cpd/.

[142] *See* Titumir, *supra* note 209; *see also* National Dialogues, *Borrowing From the IMF will Limit Bangladesh Government's Fiscal Flexibility: Remarked CPD*, CENTRE FOR POLICY DIALOGUE (February 13, 2011) http://cpd.org.bd/borrowing-from-the-imf-will-limit-bangladesh-governments-fiscal-flexibility-remarked-cpd/ (stating that "[t]he 2011 CPD study also noted that, "for a sustainable and inclusive development, Bangladesh economy needs to experience structural changes based on promotion of productive sectors, which are heavily underutilized, especially in the agricultural sector.")

[143] *See* Campaign Paper, *supra* note 207.

[144] *See* Byron & Chowhury, *supra* note 207.

[145] "After years of delays and arrangements, the Government announced that the switch to the Value Added Tax and Supplementary Duty Act, 2012, would happen from July 1, 2017." Mary Swire, *Bangladesh Confirms New Vat Law*, Corporate Tax Cuts, TAX-NEWS.COM (June 9, 2017) http://www.tax-news.com/news/Bangladesh_Confirms_New_Vat_Law_Corporate_Tax_Cuts____74438.html; *see also See* Byron & Chowhury, *supra* note 207.

[146] *See* Campaign Paper, *supra* note 207.

[147] *See* Mary Swire, Bangladesh Confirms New Vat Law, Corporate Tax Cuts, TAX-NEWS.COM (June 9, 2017) http://www.tax-news.com/news/Bangladesh_Confirms_New_Vat_Law_Corporate_Tax_Cuts____74438.html.

The government increased the price of electricity and decreased the subsidies to the power and petroleum sector. As a result of higher transportation and production costs, the cost of daily necessities has increased.[148] Consumer welfare security might be constrained as a result of raising CNG and furnace oil prices and placing a new VAT regime.[149] This would worsen the already rising economic inequality, which is of major concern for the government.[150]

In the 2017–18 national budget, Finance Minister AMA Muhith proposed Tk 2,000 crore for state-owned banks recapitalization, taking the amount to a new height of over Tk 10,000 crore since 2009.[151] Lastly, the IMF reported that, "Bangladesh benefits from lower oil prices as a net oil importer, but low oil prices could weaken job prospects for Bangladeshi workers in the gulf countries, source of two-thirds of the country's remittances."[152]

In Bangladesh, there is no mechanism to assess how much debt is tolerable and how much debt the people of Bangladesh can shoulder. Receiving these conditional loans from the IMF without any such assessment may be harmful to the whole nation.[153] Nonetheless, Bangladesh might still be entertaining more IMF conditional loan proposals in the future—another sign of the IMF's attempt to influence developing nations through free-market mechanisms.[154]

---

[148] *See* Campaign Paper, *supra* note 207.

[149] *See id.*

[150] Titumir, *supra* note 209.

[151] *See* Rejaul Karim Byron & Raez Ahmad, IMF Identifies Future Risks For Bangladesh, THE DAILY NEWS STAR (June 12, 2017) http://www.thedailystar.net/frontpage/imf-identifies-future-risks-bangladesh-1418812.

[152] *Id.*

[153] *See* Campaign Paper, *supra* note 207 (highlighting that as of March 2011, "Bangladesh's foreign debt was approximately $23,345 million, which resulted in a 20% increase in expenditures in the revenue budget. As of 2011, Bangladesh's foreign loan debt was $157 per capita.").

[154] *See id.* (noting that a "[l]oan of approximately $5bn for big construction projects, such as the Padma bridge, Deep sea port, High way road in Dhaka – Chittagong. Consequently, the per capita foreign debt would increase to approximately $202, which adversely affects the country's revenue budget and ADP implementation.").

Ghana

The World Bank's common practice of coupling its aid to low developing countries with conditions has been heavily contended and criticized by civil society organizations, governments, and academics.[155]
British and Norwegian governments have developed policies to end
the tying of their aid to privatization and liberalization conditions in
response to the Africa Commission stating that "[p]olicy conditionality
is both an infringement on sovereignty and ineffective."[156] Due to such
criticism of the conditionalities that recipient countries are pressured to
yield to, the World Bank has taken measures to reduce its conditions
per loan, on average, from an excess of forty conditions to fifteen by
2009.[157]

However, this case study on the relationship between Ghana and foreign aid banks—the World bank and IMF—will reveal that, "despite
the World Bank having decreased the average number of conditions

---

[155] See Nuria Molina, *The World Bank Failing to Deliver Real Change on Conditionality*, HOUSE
FINANCIAL SERVICES COMMITTEE 1 (June 18, 2008),
http://archives.financialservices.house.gov/hearing110/molina061808.pdf (stating that
"the Bank's use of policy conditionality and, in particular, its use of economic policy
conditionality, for being ineffective, undermining country ownership, and imposing
inappropriate policy choices.").

[156] *Id.*

[157] See Nora Honkaniemi, *Conditionality in World Bank Crisis-Lending to Ghana*, EURODAD 1
(July 2010),
http://www.eurodad.org/uploadedfiles/whats_new/reports/under%20the%20influence%
20of%20the%20world%20bank%20lay%20out.pdf; *see also World Bank and IMF Conditionality: A Development Injustice*, EURODAD 1, 8, 17 (June 2006),
http://www.eurodad.org/uploadedfiles/whats_new/reports/eurodad_world_bank_and_i
mf_conditionality_report.pdf (illustrating in Table 1 that loans to Ghana in 2005 contained fifty-two conditions and Table 4 shows Uganda suffering the most conditions of
any country at 197 conditions in 2004). "All together, these loans have 57 conditions
attached, including both binding conditions and benchmarks. This shows that, despite
the World Bank having decreased the average number of conditions per loan, some countries such as Ghana still face multiple conditions, particularly when they have several
Bank operations in place." Nora Honkaniemi, *Conditionality in World Bank Crisis-Lending
to Ghana*, EURODAD 1, 2 (July 2010),
http://www.eurodad.org/uploadedfiles/whats_new/reports/under%20the%20influence%
20of%20the%20world%20bank%20lay%20out.pdf.

per loan, some countries such as Ghana still face multiple conditions, particularly when they have several Bank operations in place."[158]

The 2008 financial and economic crisis (called by some the worst since the Great Depression of 1930) led to a global recession that left Ghana facing financial strain.[159] In order to fill the fiscal gap as a result of the crisis, the World Bank approved three loans to the country totaling $535 million: Second Natural Resources and Environmental Governance Development Policy Operation ($10 million); Transport Sector Project ($225 million); and Economic Governance and Poverty Reduction Credit ("EGPRC") ($300 million).[160] Although the combined total of loan conditions and benchmarks amount to fifty-seven, it is apparent that the World Bank has reduced the conditions in its loan agreements, only to add more conditions in separate documents.[161]

For instance, according to the Program[162] in the EGPRC Financing Agreement, Ghana has "opened a single treasury account in the Bank

---

[158] *Id.* at 2.

[159] *See id.* at 2; *see also* Mark Weisbrot et al., *IMF-Supported Macroeconomic Policies and the World Recession: A Look at Forty-One Borrowing Countries*, CENTER FOR POLICY AND ECONOMIC RESEARCH 1, 33—4 (Oct. 2009), http://cepr.net/documents/publications/imf-2009-10.pdf (stating that the IMF noted that foreign investment was not encouraging and projected private remittances to drop 30% by 2009 due to the global crisis); *The Republic of Ghana: Economic Governance and Poverty Reduction Credit*, THE WORLD BANK 1, 47 (June 15, 2009), http://documents.worldbank.org/curated/en/275321468036344421/pdf/472230PGD0P1131 01Official0Use0Only1.pdf (indicating that Ghana recorded a $941 million deficit at the end of 2008 in comparison to the $413 million surplus in 2007).

[160] *See* Nora Honkaniemi, *Conditionality in World Bank Crisis-Lending to Ghana*, EURODAD 1, 2 (July 2010), http://www.eurodad.org/uploadedfiles/whats_new/reports/under%20the%20influence%20of%20the%20world%20bank%20lay%20out.pdf (stating that, of the $535 million, $150 million would not be disbursed to the government until the completion of its commitment to the conditions in the loan).

[161] *See id.* (explaining that twelve of the fifty-seven were not made explicit in the loan agreement, but refer to a separate document, contravening the principle for responsible financing).

[162] *See* Manush A. Hristov, *Financing Agreement for Credit 4634-GH Conformed*, WASHINGTON, DC: WORLD BANK 1, 10 (July 15, 2009), http://documents.worldbank.org/curated/en/708211468250244546/Financing-Agreement-for-Credit-4634-GH-Conformed (defining Program as "actions, objectives and policies

of Ghana and has identified the MDAs'[163] accounts to be connected to the said account, in accordance with the provisions of paragraphs 36 and 37 of the Letter of Development Policy."[164] This allows foreign lenders to evade scrutiny while subjecting the less developed countries receiving loans to nearly the same restrictions and conditions.[165]

A number of the conditions in Ghana's loans reference and apply to different sectors (like energy and extraction) that should remain under the nation's control and discretion.[166] While the World Bank's focus is to increase private investment in utilities, research shows that these efforts have actually increased poverty and inequality in the country.[167]

---

designed to promote economic governance and reduce poverty and set forth or referred to in the Letter of Development Policy").

[163] *See id.* (defining MDA as the recipient countries ministries, departments, and agencies).

[164] *Id.* at 4; *see id.* at 10 (defining Letter of Development Policy as "the Recipient's letter to the Association dated June 12, 2009, declaring the Recipient's commitment to the execution of the Program and requesting assistance from the Association in support of the Program during its execution").

[165] *See* Nora Honkaniemi, *Conditionality in World Bank Crisis-Lending to Ghana*, EURODAD 1, 2 (July 2010), http://www.eurodad.org/uploadedfiles/whats_new/reports/under%20the%20influence%20of%20the%20world%20bank%20lay%20out.pdf (indicating Ghana it still subjected to numerous conditions when several World Bank operations are utilized).

[166] *See id.* at 3 (explaining that recent spikes in electricity prices, 150% and greater, are direct results from the conditions the bank imposes on Ghana pertaining to the electricity sector); *see also* Sunil Mathrani et al., *Energizing Economic Growth in Ghana: Making the Power and Petroleum Sectors Rise to the Challenge*, WASHINGTON, DC: WORLD BANK i, xx (June 1, 2013), http://documents.worldbank.org/curated/en/485911468029951116/Energizing-economic-growth-in-Ghana-making-the-power-and-petroleum-sectors-rise-to-the-challenge (indicating that the World Bank's recommended actions included a major tariff revision); Ismi, *supra* note 152. (explaining that Ghana's relationship with the World Bank and the IMF has led to over 130 privatized state enterprises, removal of tariff barriers, and the end of subsidies for health and education, resulting in a twenty percent unemployment rate for Ghanians).

[167] *See* Nora Honkaniemi, *Conditionality in World Bank Crisis-Lending to Ghana*, EURODAD 1, 3 (July 2010), http://www.eurodad.org/uploadedfiles/whats_new/reports/under%20the%20influence%20of%20the%20world%20bank%20lay%20out.pdf ("[C]ontrary to expectations, private investors have shied away from investing in such utilities in the region [and]…the focus of investors on cost recovery has not promoted social objectives, such as reducing poverty and promoting equity."). Although studies have shown changes in the World

The very purpose for reaching out to foreign aid and enduring the conditions that accompany these loans is to improve—not hinder—the country's economy; however, the poor pay more for utility services provided by privatized suppliers.[168] These conditions commit time and resources to attract private investors for utilities, and these same investors who have been reluctant in investing due to the risks involved focus on cost recovery rather than the country's economic well-being.[169]

Furthermore, in order to expedite the expansion of the private sector, the loan requires the country to implement a hiring freeze in the pubic sector.[170] Although these measures were taken in an attempt to control expenditures and reduce the fiscal deficit, it remains counterintuitive because the poor will suffer most by having to pay higher utilities cost while dealing with no job security.[171]

Bank's policy concerning privatization of water utilities, certain countries, including Ghana, serve "as examples where the World Bank continues to push its traditional privatisation policies without regard to poorer groups." Benedict Bull, *The World Bank's and the IMF's use of Conditionality to Encourage Privatization and Liberalization: Current Issues and Practices*, NORWEGIAN MINISTRY OF FOREIGN AFFAIRS 1, 26 (Nov. 2006), https://www.regjeringen.no/globalassets/upload/kilde/ud/rap/2006/0164/ddd/pdfv/30049 5-7final_conditionality_report.pdf.

[168] *See* Kate Bayliss & Terry McKinley, *Privatising Basic Utilities in Sub-Saharan Africa: The MDG Impact*, UNITED NATIONS DEVELOPMENT PROGRAMME 1, 3 (Jan. 2007), http://www.ipc-undp.org/pub/IPCPolicyResearchBrief3.pdf (illustrating in Figure 1 the global payments that are made to privately owned suppliers, which greatly exceed the payments made to public utilities). For example, in Ghana, the financial sustainability of rural services has been jeopardized. The rural areas and small towns once benefited from subsidies due to the higher tariffs imposed on the larger urban areas, but the government has eliminated these subsidies preparing for privatization. *See id.*

[169] *See Id.* at 1.

[170] *See* Nora Honkaniemi, *Conditionality in World Bank Crisis-Lending to Ghana*, EURODAD 1, 4 (July 2010), http://www.eurodad.org/uploadedfiles/whats_new/reports/under%20the%20influence% 20of%20the%20world%20bank%20lay%20out.pdf.

[171] *See Ghana - Economic Governance and Poverty Reduction Credit Program*, WASHINGTON, DC: WORLD BANK 1, 9 (June 15, 2009), http://documents.worldbank.org/curated/en/275321468036344421/Ghana-Economic-Governance-and-Poverty-Reduction-Credit-Program (stating that measures being implemented also comprised of "(i) increasing revenues…by improving VAT collection, raising airport taxes, and official grants…; (ii) compressing operational expenditures…;

Even though the World Bank has "reduced" its conditions attached to loan agreements, the Bank exerts its power and influence on the Ghanaian economy through separate documents that enforce its own conditions and requirements.[172] "An aid relationship is a negotiated contractual arrangement between unequal partners, and it is naïve to assume that conflicts of interest and divergent opinions will not exist," but to what extent should the aid donors exercise "the power of the purse?"[173] Benchmarks and conditions are common contractual practices and some are necessary to facilitate the effectiveness of aid. However, the loan conditionalities between the World Bank and Ghana fail at transparency and encroach on the country's own policy space.[174]

The latest conditions imposed by the IMF allow Ghanaian currency to depreciate, cut government spending, reduce or remove subsidies, and increase the price of utilities.[175] In 2015, Ghana confronted a sovereign debt crisis, rising interest costs, policy slippages and external shocks that have dampened the country's medium-term prospects. Further, the sacrifices the IMF wants Ghana to make have put the government's credibility on the line.[176]

(iii) postponing non-essential new investment projects...; and (iv) establishing the treasury single account to improve cash management.").

[172] *See* Nora Honkaniemi, *Conditionality in World Bank Crisis-Lending to Ghana*, EURODAD 1, 4 (July 2010), http://www.eurodad.org/uploadedfiles/whats_new/reports/under%20the%20influence%20of%20the%20world%20bank%20lay%20out.pdf.

[173] Benedict Bull, *The World Bank's and the IMF's use of Conditionality to Encourage Privatization and Liberalization: Current Issues and Practices*, NORWEGIAN MINISTRY OF FOREIGN AFFAIRS 1, 46–7 (Nov. 2006), https://www.regjeringen.no/globalassets/upload/kilde/ud/rap/2006/0164/ddd/pdfv/300495-7final_conditionality_report.pdf.

[174] *See id.* at 47; Nora Honkaniemi, *Conditionality in World Bank Crisis-Lending to Ghana*, EURODAD 1, 4 (July 2010), http://www.eurodad.org/uploadedfiles/whats_new/reports/under%20the%20influence%20of%20the%20world%20bank%20lay%20out.pdf.

[175] Vincent Nwanma, *Can Ghana Afford IMF Conditions For Loan?*, GLOBAL FINANCE MAGAZINE (September 11, 2014), http://www.gfmag.com/magazine/september-2014/can-ghana-afford-imf-conditions-loan.

[176] B&FT, *IMF Conditionalities Create Rough Road for Government*, GENERAL NEWS (April 24, 2015) https://www.ghanaweb.com/GhanaHomePage.

This places significant pressure on the government to spend within its means, since the Bank of Ghana has over the past four years been the main source of funding for the government's huge deficit. Ghana's economic growth rate topped 9% in 2011, but three difficult years followed. Slowing activity, accelerating inflation, and rising debt levels and financial vulnerabilities characterized these years.[177]

As reported by the B&FT, the IMF wants the Bank of Ghana to "completely shy away from printing money to finance government's budget -- latest by 2016 -- before which the central bank's financial assistance to the government must be limited to five percent of the previous year's revenue."[178] The IMF also pushed for a new tax policy regime to be enacted for small businesses, as well as a raise in the VAT threshold.[179]

The country's economic prospects were put at risk by the emergence of large fiscal and external imbalances, as well as electricity shortages.[180] Additionally, the IMF wants the government to eliminate subsidies for utilities and fuel consumption by ensuring implementation of the agreed automatic adjustment formula.[181] The measures seek to boost

---

[177] The IMF put Ghana into the category of countries that are a few steps away from falling into the league of High Debt Distress Countries (HDDC) after its debts in relation to taxes, revenue and exports crossed the minimum threshold that measures a country's distress status. The IMF's fiscal monitoring report projected that the country's debt-to-GDP ratio might hit the dreaded 70% by end of 2015. According to the IMF, Ghana was put into this category to ensure that any financial institution or investor dealing with Ghana appreciates and understands the country's ability to pay its debts on time. *See* B&FT, *supra* note 275.

[178] The Ghanaian government was also told by the IMF to "tame its appetite for borrowing and limit the rush to the international capital market, and [to] instead adopt a prudent borrowing strategy in order to improve the country's debt distress situation," which witnessed a debt-to-GDP ratio jump from 54.8% in 2013 to 67.2% at the end of 2014. *See id.*

[179] *Id.*

[180] *See* B B&FT, *supra* note 275.

[181] *Id.*

government revenue and raise export earnings by making the country's products cheaper, while raising the prices of imports.[182]

As of 2015, Ghana was the world's second-largest producer of cocoa.[183] With the Ghanaian cedi having lost approximately 36% of its value against the dollar in 2014, the country, also a major producer of gold, can no longer afford to delay talks with the IMF.[184] Ghana faces a trade deficit as a result of rising imports, including food items, unmatched by exports. Its main exports—cocoa and gold—have not fared well recently. Gold prices fell approximately 2% in 2013, closing at $1,200 per ounce, and recovery has been slow. After reaching an all-time high in 2011, cocoa has also experienced downward pressure.[185]

Ghana's 2014 budget deficit was estimated to be 8.5% of GDP. To reduce or eliminate this shortfall, the government may need to cut its workforce and reduce other expenses. With about 70% of state expenditure going to workers, the impact of such a cut will be significant for local economies.[186]

The impact of IMF pressures on developing countries is not limited to macroeconomics. Research shows that the IMF has exerted a "unique influence" on the evolution of health care in Ghana.[187] This is largely due to the IMF's requirements that governments adopt policies that "prioritize short-term economic objectives over long-term investments, such as in the healthcare system," in exchange for these conditionality loans.[188] Though the Ghanaian healthcare system was weak before the IMF got involved due to conflicts and national political unrest, the IMF

---

[182] *See supra* note 27 and accompanying text.
[183] *See supra* note 27 and accompanying text.
[184] *See supra* note 27 and accompanying text.
[185] *Id.*
[186] *Id.*
[187] Thomas Stubbs & Alexander E. Kentikelenis, *How Years of IMF Prescriptions Have Hurt West African Health Systems*, THE CONVERSATION (February 22, 2017) https://theconversation.com/how-years-of-imf-prescriptions-have-hurt-west-african-health-systems-72806.
[188] *Id.*

has, for the last twenty years, set the fiscal and institutional constraints within which health-related policies develop.

Yet, the IMF's policy reform demands over these past two decades in exchange for loan disbursements have not fixed the problem.[189] Not only have they undermined the Ghanaian government's ability to repair its historic problems, but they may have also weakened Ghana's chance at sustainable development and growth in the long term.[190]

The IMF diverts government expenditure on public health and deflects resources from the health sector to pay off the country's incurred debt.[191] Also, "macroeconomic targets set by the IMF reduced fiscal space for health investment."[192] Public health spending still remains minimal at 2.4% of the GDP in 2014; and infant mortality rates are among the highest worldwide, with a regional average of 57.8 deaths per 1,000 live births in 2015.[193] The IMF also pushes for decentralization of health-related services, which rather than making such services more amenable to local needs, debilitates the delivery of suitable healthcare to the people.[194]

For example, some loan conditions specified wage and personnel caps that in turn limited staff expansion of medical professionals. These fiscal caps consequently limited the ability of clinics and hospitals to employ sufficient medical professionals.[195] In 2005, a series of IMF conditions sought to reduce Ghana's public-sector wage bill. The Ghanaian Minister of Finance wrote to the IMF that "at the current level of remuneration, the civil service is losing highly productive employees, par-

---

[189] Id.
[190] Id.
[191] Id.
[192] Thomas Stubbs & Alexander E. Kentikelenis, *How Years of IMF Prescriptions Have Hurt West African Health Systems*, THE CONVERSATION (February 22, 2017) https://theconversation.com/how-years-of-imf-prescriptions-have-hurt-west-african-health-systems-72806.
[193] Id.
[194] Id.
[195] Id.

ticularly in the health sector."[196] These wage and personnel caps stayed in place until the end of 2006, which reduced by 50% the number of physicians in Ghana.[197]

Many public health practitioners and experts in the region believe that the IMF contributed to the failure of health systems in Ghana to develop into effective and sustainable mechanisms in the service of public health. Preventing the system's development might have exacerbated the Ebola crisis of 2014.[198] Administrative reforms, such as IMF's advised decentralization of budgetary responsibilities from the central government to the regional level in the early 2000s, prevented the delivery of satisfactory health care to the public, especially to those vulnerable populations who required acute care.[199] The health care system in Ghana is but one example of the need for the IMF and World Bank to reform in a way that advances sustainable development not entirely focused on free market priorities.

---

[196] *Id.*

[197] *Id.*

[198] Thomas Stubbs & Alexander E. Kentikelenis, *How Years of IMF Prescriptions Have Hurt West African Health Systems*, THE CONVERSATION (February 22, 2017) https://theconversation.com/how-years-of-imf-prescriptions-have-hurt-west-african-health-systems-72806.

[199] *Id.*

MORE INTERNATIONAL CHALLENGES

Challenge of the Monterrey Consensus

I n 2002, the BWI conjured a recipe of false hope through their participation in and subsequent lack of commitment to the Monterrey Consensus ("Consensus").[1] Prior to the Consensus, the World Bank was criticized because many of its low-interest loans went to corrupt governments that were not held responsible when money could not be accounted for.[2] The IMF was criticized for its expensive rescue operations, and for giving too little attention to improving financial structures in developing countries.[3]

---

[1] *Forging the Monterrey Consensus*, N.Y. TIMES (Mar. 24, 2002) http://www.nytimes.com/2002/03/24/opinion/forging-the-monterrey-consensus.html (explaining criticisms aimed at the World Bank and other international development bodies because the aid doled out by those institutions to countries made no great progress in those countries at eliminating poverty); *See also* Susanne Soederberg, *Recasting Neoliberal Dominance in the Global South? A Critique of the Monterrey Consensus*, ALTERNATIVES: GLOBAL, LOCAL, POL., Vol. 30, No. 3, 325, 340 (July-Sept. 2005) (explaining how the World Bank found a seventy–three percent failure rate in Africa); *see also id.* (explaining the Monterrey Consensus conference). The Monterrey Consensus set a priority for combating corruption at all levels, reaffirmed at the Doha Conference. *See Draft Outcome Document on the Follow-up International Conference on Financing for Development to Review the Implementation of the Monterrey Consensus Submitted by the President of the General Assembly in Accordance with General Assembly Resolution 62/187: Doha Outcome Document on Reviewing the Implementation of the Monterrey Consensus*, UNITED NATIONS (July 28, 2008), http://www.un.org/esa/ffd/doha/draftoutcome/DraftOutcomeDoc_English.pdf [hereinafter *"General Assembly Resolution 62/187"*].

[2] *Forging the Monterrey Consensus*, *supra* note 1 at 333, 341.

[3] *See Financing for Development: Building on Monterrey*, UNITED NATIONS 9 (2002), http://www.un.org/esa/ffd/documents/Building%20on%20Monterrey.pdf [hereinafter

The Consensus sought to establish a common ground for developed and developing countries to converge in an effort to stabilize and grow the global economy in pursuit of the former MDG development objectives.[4] The atmosphere leading into Monterrey was the result of several factors: the 1997 economic crisis in South East Asia;[5] international financial institutions ("IFI") were not acting as neutral and independent public authorities; the Consensus' precursor, the Washington Consensus,[6] was "not solely political in nature, but had its roots in the changing nature of the world economy;"[7] and "growing protectionism, uni-

referred to as "*Building on Monterrey*"]. As a result, the IMF attempted reorganization in its fight against poverty with lowering demands for loan approval. *Id.; see* M.L. NARA-SAIAH, MICROCREDIT AND RURAL POVERTY 103–04 (Discovery Publ'g House) (2006) (explaining that structural-adjustment programs were replaced by Poverty-Reduction Strategy Papers).

[4] The Consensus contains six thematic "chapters" for action, including one devoted to external-debt-relief. *See Building on Monterrey, supra* note 3, at VII–X.

[5] *See id.;* Akila Weerapana, *Lecture 23: The IMF and Its Critics, Spring 2003 & 2004*, WELLESLEY, https://www.coursehero.com/file/7127599/IMF-Ch23/ (last visited Nov. 23, 2017). Following the East Asia crisis, the IMF imposed conditions on the Indonesian government to get fiscal spending under control. *Id.* Rather than using financial aid to put an end to widespread corruption, the Indonesian government was forced to remove food and fuel subsidies, a blow to the poor in Jakarta. *Id.* The IMF was further criticized for allowing devaluation to occur, stating this was the catalyst to the crisis. *Id.* The IMF should be helping countries defend their currencies, rather than devaluing them. *Id.* The IMF required high interest rates in exchange for bailouts. *Id.; see* Paul Blustein, *World Bank Turns Up Criticism of the IMF*, WASH. POST (Dec. 3, 1998), http://www.globalpolicy.org/component/content/article/209/43528.html (last visited on Nov. 23, 2017). Although the institutions usually work in tandem, the World Bank lending for long-term and the IMF short-term relief, this rift marked a growing separation between Europe and the United States of America. *General Assembly Resolution 62/187, supra* note 1.

[6] Soederberg, *supra* note 1 (explaining the Washington Consensus as the neo–liberalistic policy of the IFIs, such as the IMF and World Bank, that believed political and social problems should not be solved through state intervention and instead through market-based mechanisms).

[7] *See* Soederberg, *supra* note 1 (discussing three caveats leading to the Monterrey consensus). The heavily skewed IMF voting power and United States dominance within the World Bank's standby capital were examples of how IFIs are not natural and independent authorities. *See id.* The roots of the Washington consensus being in the changing nature of the economy meant that policies were created as a reaction to the crisis of overproduction and thus there was a growing dependence of corporations, governments, and consumers on debt financing. *See id.* Finally, the policies of the Bush administration led to overproduction because performance-based grants were intrinsically tied to the efforts

lateralism, and fiscal overrun pursued by the Bush administration" created a crisis of overproduction, which was not simply a reaction to the events of September 11, 2001.[8]

Preparation for the Consensus spanned four years of "patient consensus-building work."[9] By the end of the fourth preparatory meeting for the Monterrey Conference, all participants endorsed the Monterrey Consensus.[10] The Zedillo report,[11] prepared by a panel of the world's

---

to maintain U.S. competitiveness and dominant position in the world economy. *See id.* Thus, tax cuts and government spending, coupled with a fear of public backlash by policymakers wary of criticizing the administration's budget, led to a rise in debt levels. *See id.*

[8] *Calls Heard for Increased Aid to Reduce Poverty at Monterrey Conference on Development Financing*, UNITED NATIONS (Mar. 21, 2002), http://www.un.org/ffd/pressrel/21c.htm (explaining how September 11 tore down the invisible wall dividing rich and poor worldwide) [hereinafter "Calls Heard for Aid"]. The Monterrey Conference should serve to rebuild confidence lost in the international economy and system as a result of 9/11/01 events. *See id.*; *Group of 77 Plays Key Role in Monterrey Consensus on FFD*, G77, http://www.g77.org/news/monterrey.htm (last visited Aug. 19, 2017) [hereinafter *Group of 77*]. "Greater confidence should lead to higher investments and stronger recovery as well as concrete measures in international trade and better prices for primary commodities." *Id.* Since then, re-development in the world's poorest societies as taken on a sense of urgency because "although not a direct cause of terrorism, 'poverty breeds frustration and resentment . . . particularly in those countries in which poverty is coupled with a lack of political rights and basic freedoms.'" *See Calls Heard for Aid, supra* note 8; *see* Lan Cao, *Cultural Change*, 47 VA. J. INT'L L. 357, 363 (2007) (citing Colin Powell, *No Country Left Behind*, FOREIGN POL'Y Jan.-Feb. 2005, at 30).

[9] *Building on Monterrey, supra* note 3, at vii. The Paris Club has since become a highly-popular bilateral institution supplying multiple avenues of debt relief to many low-income developing countries. *See generally Club de Paris*, PARIS CLUB (last visited Nov.23, 2017), http://www.clubdeparis.org/en/. Under most administrations, a common thread has been the identification and focus on enhancing long–term development goals. *See* JOHN R. ERIKSSON, *TOWARD COUNTRY–LED DEVELOPMENT: A MULTI-PARTNER EVALUATION OF THE COMPREHENSIVE DEVELOPMENT FRAMEWORK 25* (The International Bank for Reconstruction and Development / The World Bank, 2003). Nations were encouraged to lead a strong commitment and ownership of national strategies. *Id.*

[10] *See* Ernesto Zedillo, *Report of the High-Level Panel on Financing for Development*, U.N. (Jun. 26, 2001), http://www.un.org/esa/ffd/a55-1000.pdf [hereinafter referred to as "Zedillo Report"]. At the time, it was believed that the MDGs could only be reached if developed countries increased aid by $50 billion dollars per year. *Id.*

[11] Barbara Crossette, *No Headline*, N.Y. TIMES (Jul. 1, 2001), http://www.nytimes.com/2001/07/01/world/no-headline-545066.html?mcubz=1 (discussing the recommendations put forth in the Zedillo report as setting an objective of free trade to take place between industrial and developing countries, as it already had between industrial countries); Zedillo Report, *supra* note 10 (describing the key issues in the

leading financial and development experts,[12] was reviewed by the preparatory committee and indicated that restructuring the international financial architecture was a crucial issue in meeting the former MDG.[13]

External-debt relief, in addition to other goals and challenges of financing for development, was not a novel idea to the heads of State and Government at the international conference[14] in Monterrey, Mexico.[15] External debt damaged countries by consuming resources that could be used for public services and poverty eradication.[16] Thus, the focal point of the development committee's meeting at Monterrey was ensuring commitment to lifting more people from poverty and allowing them to reap benefits associated with globalization and economic development.[17] The challenging plan set forth by the BWI involved com-

---

Zedillo Report, which include mobilizing domestic financial resources, foreign investment, trade, official development assistant (ODA), external debt and the international financial architecture); *see also* World Bank and IMF Roles Debated at Development Finance Summit, http://www.brettonwoodsproject.org/art-16170 (Mar. 25, 2005).
[12] *Id.*
[13] *See Development Finance Summit a Fiasco: Say Campaigners*, BRETTON WOODS PROJECT (Mar. 25, 2002), http://www.brettonwoodsproject.org/2002/03/art-16172/ [hereinafter referred to as "Development Finance Summit"].
[14] The summit marked the culmination of four years of "patient consensus-building work." *See* Soren Ambrose, *Social Movements and the Politics of Debt Cancellation*, 6 Chi. J. Int'l L. 267.
[15] *Building on Monterrey, supra* note 3, at vii (explaining that the heads of State and Government met March 18–22, 2002 in Monterrey, Mexico to discuss and finalize implementation of the Consensus).
[16] *See Building on Monterrey, supra* note 3, at 25. "We must do our utmost to ensure that people at the local level understand this process, are engaged, and have the means to take advantage of its opportunities." *See id.* Criticism at the NGO Global forum stated "Monterrey . . . is an example of the negative impacts of globalization on people, particularly the high social costs of production of the large–scale enterprises." *See id.* at 307. Rather than focusing on privatization and neo-liberal tactics, which incur substantial micro-economic harms, the focus should be on developing world-wide economy based on human rights and environmental protections. *See id.*
[17] *See* Trevor Manuel, *Remarks at the International Conference on Financing for Development* U.N. (Mar. 18, 2002), http://www.un.org/ffd/statements/cdcE.htm; *see also Making Globalization Work for All*, UNDP (last visited Nov. 23, 2017), http://www.undp.org/content/dam/undp/library/corporate/UNDP-in-action/2007/UNDP-in-action-2007-en-.pdf?download. Chairman Manuel noted that although the consensus for cooperation between developed and developing countries were strong, so was the risk of failing to implement the Consensus. *Id.* The BWI's envision

mandeering globalization to advance the goal of poverty reduction.[18] Chairman Trevor Manuel stated that "[r]eform of international financial governance is critical to ensuring that developing countries benefit from globalization through participation."[19] Challenges in achieving debt-relief changed institutional objectives from "achieving a permanent exit from debt rescheduling . . . to removing the debt overhang within a reasonable time and providing a base from which to achieve debt sustainability."[20]

Since the cornerstone of the former MDG was halving poverty,[21] the primary focus in formulating the Consensus was to address the commonly occurring "shortfalls in resources required to achieve the internationally agreed development goals, including those contained in the United Nations Millennium Declaration (the "Declaration")."[22] At the conference, the "performance-driven aid"[23] initiative was heavily supported through the two-tiered lending structure of the Highly Indebted

---

globalization as the solution to poverty, and their neo–liberal practices as its antidote. *See* Joseph Yu, *Has Globalization eased global poverty?* CHOIKE.ORG, (Aug. 2005), http://www.choike.org/nuevo_eng/informes/3316.html. The BWI claim ineffective integration of low-income countries rather than globalization has caused the onslaught of global poverty. *See id.* "Although globalization brought overall net benefits and was also contributing to poverty reduction, its growth effects were unequally distributed, and so far it had contributed little to greater gender equality. As a result, progress towards the former Millennium Development Goals differed considerably across regions and countries." *Id.; see Globalization, Development, and Poverty Reduction–Their Social and Gender Dimensions*, U.N. (last visited May 15, 2017), http://www.un.org/webcast/unctad/xii/pdf/talking_point_rt1.pdf. *See also supra* Chapter I note 21 and accompanying text.

[18] *See* Manuel, *supra* note 17; *see also Making Globalization Work for All, supra* note 17.
[19] *Remarks at the International Conference on Financing for Development, supra* note 17. *See* A. GESKE DIJKSTRA, THE IMPACT OF INTERNATIONAL DEBT RELIEF 107 (2007).
[20] *Id.*
[21] *Calls Heard for Aid, supra* note 8.
[22] *See Monterrey Consensus of the International Conference on Financing for Development*, UNITED NATIONS (2002), http://www.un.org/esa/ffd/monterrey/MonterreyConsensus.pdf.
[23] Sophie Smyth & Anna Triponel, *Development Goals and Indicators: Education as a Lynchpin for Development: Legal and Policy Considerations in the Formation of Education for All – Fast Track Catalytic Trust Fund*, 6 SUSTAINABLE DEV. L. & POL'Y 8, 8 (2005) (stating "international development aid should follow and support clear evidence of commitment to reform and improvement on the part of the recipient country.").

Poor Countries Initiative (the "HIPC").[24] The Consensus also called for international financial institutions and bilateral agencies[25] to "scale-up." The main emphasis was "broadening and strengthening the role of developing countries in international economic decision-making and norm setting."[26]

Crucial to this objective was a financial structure and system that could be beneficial, purposeful, and feasible in facilitating the stated 21st-century values.[27] The Consensus sought the formulation of a "new partnership between developed and developing countries,"[28] fueled by the fundamental values expressed in the Declaration.[29] It promoted the values of freedom, equality, solidarity, tolerance, respect for nature, and shared responsibility[30] as essential for survival in the 21st century international arena.

---

[24] See Debt Relief Under the Heavily Indebted Poor Countries (HIPC) Initiative, INT'L MONETARY FUND (Apr. 17, 2017), http://www.imf.org/external/np/exr/facts/hipc.htm; see also The Heavily Indebted Poor Countries Initiative, THE WORLD BANK, (last visited Aug. 20, 2017) http://go.worldbank.org/XLE8KKLEX0.

[25] Building on Monterrey, supra note 3, at 3.

[26] Haque & Burdescu, supra Chapter I note 17.

[27] United Nations Millennium Declaration, G.A. Res. 55/2, U.N. GAOR, 55th Sess., Supp. No. 49, at 4, U.N. Doc. A/55/49 (2000), http://www.un.org/millennium/declaration/ares552e.htm (last visited May 15, 2017) [hereinafter Millennium Declaration]. Development and poverty eradication "depends on good governance at the international level and on transparency in the financial, monetary and trading systems." Id. "We are committed to an open, equitable, rule-based, predictable and non–discriminatory multilateral trading and financial system." Id. See Report of the International Conference of Financing for Development, UNITED NATIONS (last visited Aug. 20, 2017), http://www.ipu.org/splz-e/ffd08/monterrey.pdf.

[28] Financing For Development: Revisiting The Monterrey Consensus, INTERNATIONAL MONETARY FUND (July 2015), http://www.imf.org/external/np/pp/eng/2015/061515.pdf. The declaration was a re–affirmation of the original charter of the United Nations. Millennium Declaration, supra note 27. In addition to the original principles of human dignity, equality, and equity, the Millennium Declaration sought to expand their perspective to ascertain the needs of a developing global economy. See id.

[29] See id. "Responsibility for managing worldwide economic and social development, as well as threats to international peace and security, must be shared among the nations of the world and should be exercised multilaterally." See id. "As the most universal and most representative organization in the world, the United Nations must play the central role." See id.

[30] See Building on Monterrey, supra note 3, at 4.

"Sustainable debt financing is an important element for mobilizing re-sources for public and private investment."[31] The Consensus promoted the idea of accountability, stating "[d]ebtor and creditor countries should be mutually responsible for preventing and resolving un-sustainable debt situations."[32] The BWI' critical role, in addition to fa-cilitating lending venues, was to provide "technical assistance for ex-ternal debt management and debt tracking."[33]

Several opinions regarding the facilitation of worldwide debt reduction were presented at the Consensus.[34] The developed nations and devel-oping countries differed on how to reduce debt. Norway's Prime Min-ister Kjell Magne Bondevik informed delegates that the Norwegian government planned to increase official development assistance from .92% to 1% of GDP by 2005, advance policy coherence, and forgive all debts to countries under the HIPC.[35]

Most donor countries only provided 0.22% of GDP, with only five countries reaching the 0.70% target.[36] Former U.S. President George W. Bush proposed, "[D]evelopment resources should be distributed fifty percent for grants and fifty percent for loans."[37] The approach to can-

---

[31] *See id.* at 9.

[32] *See id.* at 219.

[33] *See Building on Monterrey, supra* note 3, at 9.

[34] *See Calls Heard for Aid, supra* note 8.

[35] *See id.* By the rate at which it was improving at the time of the conference, the ODA would only reach 0.7% in 2032. *See id.* The European Union was only contributing 0.27%, pledging to increase its contribution to 0.39% at the EU Barcelona Summit. *See id.; see Small Steps Towards More Development Aid: Financing for Development Conference Finishes in Monterrey,* OUTREACH 2002 (Mar. 25, 2002), www.earthsummit2002.org/es/newsletter/Issue%2020.pdf.

[36] *See Calls Heard for Aid, supra* note 8. Proposed increase in development assistance by the United States was projected to reach "a $5 Billion annual increase over current lev-els." *See Building on Monterrey, supra* note 3, at 113; *see also* Stephen Marks, *U.S. Foreign Policy and Human Rights: The Human Right to Development: Between Rhetoric and Reality,* 17 HARV. HUM. RTS. J. 137, 156–57 (2004) (discussing Bush's speech at Monterrey). Bush said that developed nations had duties to share wealth and encourage sources that produce wealth such as economic freedom, human rights, rule of law, and political liberty. *Id.*

[37] *Id.*

cellation of debts expressed by NGOs attending the conference was heavily ignored.[38]

Developing countries held strong views about how poverty reduction should have been accomplished.[39] Small island nations pushed for the international community to expand the HIPC.[40] African developing countries stressed that since most of their economies were based on exporting, the deterioration of trade had a negative impact on the balance of payments and, thus, economic growth.[41] Donald Kaberuka, Rwanda's Minister for Financing and Economic Planning, stressed that aid alone would not eliminate poverty and that there should be greater integration of poor countries into world-wide trade and investment.[42]

---

[38] *See generally* Laura Frade, *NGO Global Forum*, UNITED NATIONS (Mar. 18, 2002) http://www.un.org/ffd/statements/ngoE.htm. "[A] fair and transparent process of arbitration" should be used to cancel "external debt of countries of the south." *Id.* "All forms of conditionality should be eliminated, such as tied aid, and food aid, which undermines the productive capacity, and food security of countries." *Id. See World Economic Outlook: Database – WEO Groups and Aggregates Information*, INT'L MONETARY FUND (Oct. 2009), http://www.imf.org/external/pubs/ft/weo/2009/02/weodata/groups.htm#oem (listing emerging and developing economies as well as advanced economies).

[39] *See* Gaston Browne, *Statement at the International Conference on Finance for Development*, UNITED NATIONS (Mar. 22, 2002), http://www.un.org/ffd/statements/aabE.htm (explaining how developing countries wanted to make sure the Consensus would catapult developed countries into action instead of being just another "talk shop"); *see also* Eduardo Duhalde, *Statement at International Conference on Financing for Development*, UNITED NATIONS (Mar. 21, 2002), http://www.un.org/ffd/statements/argentinaE.htm (stating: "the gap between many emerging economies and developed countries has not been reduced[,] and [o]n the contrary, it seems deeper day by day").

[40] WORLD DEVELOPMENT INDICATORS, 11, 13 (The World Bank, 2007) (explaining that small island developing nations have special needs due to their particularly difficult geographic constraints, such as a small tax base, lack of natural resources, lack of access to ODA, substantially reduced foreign direct investment flows, and a lack of access to capital markets; several of these needs were addressed "through the Programme of Action for the Sustainable Development of Small Island Developing States and the 22nd special session of the General Assembly.").

[41] *Calls Heard for Aid*, *supra* note 8 (discussing how creating sound environments, frameworks for investment, structural and government reforms, and transparency are all primary responsibilities of developing countries and aid should be secondary).

[42] Altai Efendiev, *Statement to the International Conference on Financing for Development at Monterrey, Mexico*, UNITED NATIONS (Mar. 21, 2002), http://www.un.org/ffd/statements/azerbaijanE.htm.

To achieve the development objectives, including the former MDGs, the U.N. members and the representatives from the BWI addressed six areas of financing for development that ultimately would become known as the Monterrey Consensus:

- the mobilization of domestic financial resources for development;[43]
- the mobilization of international resources for development through foreign direct investment and other private flows;[44]
- international trade as an engine for development;[45]

Handling and managing the expected massive inflows of resources in a most efficient way, transform potentially high growth into sustainable development is one of the major challenges...building up adequate institutional infrastructure, enhancing institutional capacities, introducing good-governance practices, pursuing radical structural and administrative reforms, implementing poverty reduction strategy, SME and non-oil sector development are ...the areas where the international assistance and expertise is most needed.
Id.

[43] *See Building on Monterrey, supra* note 3, at VIII. "In our common pursuit of growth, poverty eradication and sustainable development, a critical challenge is to ensure the necessary internal conditions for mobilizing domestic savings, both public and private, sustaining adequate levels of productive investment and increasing human capacity." *See id.* at 4. "An enabling domestic environment is vital for mobilizing domestic resources, increasing productivity, reducing capital flight, encouraging the private sector, and attracting and making effective use of international investment and assistance." *See id.* at 4. "We recognize the need to strengthen and develop the domestic financial sector, by encouraging the orderly development of capital markets . . . addressing development financing needs, including the insurance sector and debt and equity markets." *See id.* at 4.

[44] *See id.* at 5. "We will support new public/private sector financing mechanisms, both debt and equity for developing countries and countries with economies in transition." *See id.* at 6. *See* Abdel H. Bouab, Comment, *Financing for Development, the Monterrey Consensus: Achievements and Prospects,* 26 MICH. J. INT'L L. 359, 361 (2004). "Both domestic and international conditions are necessary to facilitate direct investment flows to Least Developed Countries ('LDCs')." *See Review of the Monterrey Consensus on Financing for Development,* UNITED NATIONS (Feb. 15, 2008), http://www.un.org/esa/ffd/doha/chapter2/USA_submission.pdf (stating each country is primarily responsible for maintaining its own economic environment and international institution support should be considered secondary). Although the benefits of foreign direct investment include "(1) increase in employment, (2) technological spill-overs, (3) higher public revenue, and (4) a positive impact on growth . . . such benefits may be offset by negative long-term balance-of-payments effects." David Woodward, *Foreign Direct Investment for Development?*, G–24,1, (last visited Aug. 20, 2017) https://www.g24.org/wp-content/uploads/2016/01/G24-Policy-Brief-23.pdf. "A clear distinction needs to be made between maximizing FDI flows and maximizing their contribution to development" in order to make effective use of funds. *Id.* at 2.

- increasing international financial and technical cooperation for development;[46]

- external debt;[47] and

- addressing systemic issues, including enhancement of the coherence and consistency of the international monetary, financial, and trading systems in support of development.[48]

The ability of the BWI to contribute in these areas--and particularly the sixth one which touches precisely on economic governance--was crucial to their viability.[49]

---

[45] *See Building on Monterrey, supra* note 3, at 6. Trade is the "single most important external source of development financing." *See id.* "We urge international financial institutions, including regional development banks, to continue to support projects that promote sub-regional and regional integration among developing countries and countries with economies in transition…we invite multilateral and bilateral financial and development institutions to expand and coordinate their efforts." *See id.* at 7; *see* Bouab, *supra* note 44, at 362.

[46] *See Building on Monterrey, supra* note 3, at 8. "We recognize that a substantial increase in ODA and other resources will be required if developing countries are to achieve the internationally agreed development goals and objectives, including those contained in the Millennium Declaration." *See id.* "There is a need for the multilateral…development institutions to intensify efforts to … enhance the absorptive capacity and financial management of the recipient countries…[and] enhance recipient countries' input into and ownership of the design, including procurement, of technical assistance programs." *See id.; see* Bouab, *supra* note 44, at 363.

[47] *See Building on Monterrey, supra* note 3, at 9. "External debt relief can play a key role in liberating resources that can then be directed towards activities consistent with attaining sustainable growth and development." *See id.*

[48] *See id.; see* Bouab, *supra* note 44, at 365; UNITED NATIONS ECON. AND SOC. COUNCIL, ECON. AND SOC. COMM'N FOR ASIA AND THE PAC., *Date, Venue and Theme Topic for the Sixty-First Session of the Commission*, http://www.unescap.org/60/E/E1327e.pdf (last visited Nov. 23, 2017). Commentators have suggested these six themes can actually be merged into four: "(a) bringing about a substantial increase in the volume and effectiveness of foreign resource flows (private, bilateral, and multilateral) in support of development, with a clear focus on poverty eradication; (b) setting up a fair, transparent, and ethical procedure and institutional framework for resolving external debt problems; (c) improving global economic governance to make it more participatory and accountable to a broader community of nations; and (d) creating an international trading environment that is more supportive of growth, in general, and the development of the poor, in particular." Haque & Burdescu, *supra* note 17.

[49] *See* Latin American and Caribbean Economic System (SELA), THE MONTERREY CONSENSUS SIX YEARS LATER AND FINANCING FOR DEVELOPMENT IN LATIN AMERICA AND THE CARIBBEAN 9 (June 20, 2008),

With public skepticism looming,[50] early criticisms regarding Monterrey included that it did not call for independent external evaluations of the performance of either the World Bank or the IMF,[51] and few initiatives were substantially generated to achieve the former MDG.[52] Further, insufficient attention was given to reforming the international financial institutions' composition and decision-making process of the executive boards in dealing with debt relief.[53]

In response to criticisms, IMF Managing Director, Horst Köehler, proclaimed the underlying stigma of the new plan: "nothing will work without good governance."[54] Under the HIPC, the IMF would contrib-

---

http://citeseerx.ist.psu.edu/viewdoc/download;jsessionid=895944390CB3E8F218C07ABFE 6F7FB97?doi=10.1.1.174.6295&rep=rep1&type=pdf (last visited May 15, 2017). "A real reform of the Bretton Woods Institutions is necessary…[t]he boards of directors of these institutions must be restructured so as to increase the number of seats for least developed countries." *Id.* at 23. Others have stated the UN, rather than the BWI should take charge in restructuring worldwide finances. *Id.; see* Tayob, *U.N. Only Legitimate Body to Reform Financial System*, CHOIKE.ORG (Nov. 24, 2008), http://www.choike.org/nuevo_eng/informes/7162.html (last visited Nov. 23, 2017).

[50] *See Development Finance Summit, supra* note 13 (explaining the skepticism as the product of the Monterrey Consensus being drafted in preparatory committees, and not being subject to any further negotiations). Thus, the predetermined nature of the Conference caused many civil society organizations to question their own, what was then, upcoming participation in the Conference. *See id.*

[51] *See Assessment of the FfD Outcome Paper and Proposed Next Steps*, BRETTON WOODS PROJECT (Mar. 25, 2002), http://www.brettonwoodsproject.org/2002/03/art-16171/; *See generally* INDEPENDENT EVALUATIONS OFFICE (last visited Aug. 20, 2017), http://www.ieo-imf.org/ieo/pages/ieohome.aspx [hereinafter IEO] (discussing the IMF's Independent Evaluation Office ("IEO")). The IEO was established in 2001 "to conduct independent and objective evaluations of Fund policies and activities." *Id.* The IEO is fully independent of IMF management and operates at arm's length from the Executive Directors. *Id.* The IEO's mission is to "[e]nhance the learning culture within the Fund, [s]trengthen the Fund's external credibility, [p]romote greater understanding of the work of the fund, and [s]upport institutional governance and oversight." *Id.*

[52] *See Development Finance Summit, supra* note 13 (explaining that civil society groups organized Foro Global, ahead of the Conference, to challenge the Monterrey Consensus). The Consensus was chastised for failing to propose any new ways to mobilize finances toward achieving the former MDGs. *See id.*

[53] *See* Assessment of the FfD, *supra* note 51.

[54] Horst Köehler, *Introductory Remarks at the International Conference on Financing for Development*, UNITED NATIONS (Mar. 18, 2002), http://www.un.org/ffd/statements/imfE.htm (stating poor countries should be ready to confront responsibility to their people before the international community can step in to bail them out); *Horst Köhler: Biographical In-*

ute rehabilitation and stimulus loans once the poor countries took certain measures in evaluating and formulating their domestic policies.[55] Priorities included trade, a standard of 0.7 percent GNP for debt assistance, debt relief, and institutional capacity.[56]

With 25 years of failed structural adjustment programs for poverty reduction, and with its inability to assist major countries out of poverty crisis,[57] the IMF might not be in a strong position to control the administration of such funds towards developing counties. However, it is fair to recognize, given the traditional opposition of industrial countries to discuss international financial and monetary matters in a UN setting, the Monterrey Conference, and the resulting Consensus, constituted an unprecedented blueprint for action that would bring the Bretton Woods agencies, historically dominated just by Finance Ministries, much closer to broader political decision makers.

---

formation, INT'L MONETARY FUND (last visited Aug. 20, 2017), http://www.imf.org/external/np/omd/bios/hk.htm (stating Horst Köhler served as Germany's Deputy Minister of Finance from 1990 to 1993.). During that time, he led negotiations on behalf of the German government on the Maastricht treaty. *Id.* He was President of the German Savings Bank Association from 1993 to 1998, and in September 1998, he was appointed President of the European Bank for Reconstruction and Development. *Id.* From May 2000 to March 2004 Köhler served as the Managing Director of the International Monetary Fund. *Id.*

[55] Rick Rowden, *A World of Debt: Why "Debt Relief" has Failed to Liberate Poor Countries*, AM. PROSPECT, July 1, 2001, at 29, http://www.thirdworldtraveler.com/Reforming_System/World_of_Debt.html (last visited Nov. 23, 2017) (criticizing the HIPC initiative). Although the HIPC framework invites NGOs and civic groups to consult with governments, there are not any clear guidelines as to how a legitimate NGO can be identified. *Id.* Governments in some countries had the ability to handpick who was allowed to participate in the poverty reduction process. *Id.* Legitimate NGOs have called this process a joke. *Id.*

[56] *Id.* Even the IMF doubted its capacity to provide assistance to poor countries. *Id.* A draft resolution by the economic and financial committee, in a follow-up meeting to the Monterrey Consensus held in 2005, urged for time tables to stage increments for developed countries to achieve 0.7% GDP, reaching 0.5% by 2010. *See Press Release, United Nations, Second Comm. Approves Draft Resolution Underlying Need to Improve Commitments of Monterrey Consensus*, UNITED NATIONS INFORMATION SERVICE (Dec. 20, 2005), http://www.unis.unvienna.org/unis/pressrels/2005/gaef3141.html.

[57] *See IMF Support for Low-Income Countries*, INT'L MONETARY FUND (last updated Oct. 2016), http://www.imf.org/external/np/exr/facts/poor.htm.

Challenge of Heavily Indebted Poor Countries

In response to criticism of their development approach and structural-adjustment policies, the BWI ended an eleven-year productivity drought with the formation of the HIPC.[58] With its establishment in 1996 and doubling in 1999, the HIPC provides comprehensive debt-relief[59] assistance to countries qualified to receive aid from the International Development Association (the "IDA"). [60]

To eliminate poverty, the mission was to promote local government spending on public services such as healthcare and education, and for relief to include multi-lateral creditors, such as the IMF and World Bank.[61] Unfortunately, commentators correctly predicted real

---

[58] *See* Barbara P. Thomas-Slayter, Southern Exposure: International Development and the Global South in the Twenty-First Century (2003) (discussing how the HIPC doubled through the Enhanced HIPC Initiative). For the World Bank's description of the HIPC and links to the HIPC At-A-Glance Guide and Status of Implementation *see (HIPC) The Enhanced Heavily Indebted Poor Countries Initiative*, The World Bank, http://go.worldbank.org/85B908KVE0 (last visited Nov. 23, 2017).

[59] *See* Leonie F. Guder, The Administration of Debt Relief by International Financial Institutions: A Legal Reconstruction of the HIPC Initiative 2 (2009) (defining debt relief as "a restructuring of debt that contains an element of forgiveness or reduction, thus relieving the overall debt burden of a country"). Although providing relief, as opposed to extending loans, is a drastic turn from concessional lending structures of the past, the HIPC conditions ultimately reveal similar development goals. *Id.* at 28–29. In addition to the World Bank and IMF, there are eighteen lenders affiliated with the HIPC. *See id.* at 48. The debts relieved are "official debts" because they are owed by governments or state-owned enterprises. *Id.* Half of the debt relief will be provided by bilateral funding and the other cancelled by the BWI. *Id.* at 49.

[60] *See* Thomas-Slayter, *supra* note 58, at 175 (discussing that qualification includes an unsustainable debt burden, limited exports, low foreign currency reserves, and other limited resources). Of the qualified countries, 80% are in Africa. *See id.; see also* Chapter IV for regional case studies involving countries which qualify for the HIPC.

[61] *See* Sanjee Gupta et al., *Bulletin of the World Health Organization*, Scielo Public Health (last visited Nov. 23, 2017), http://www.scielosp.org/scielo.php?script=sci_arttext&pid=S0042-96862002000200011 (discussing fiscal policy issues related to debt relief in twenty-three countries that reached their decision point under the HIPC framework).

debt relief provided by the HIPC would be substantially lower than anticipated.[62]

The BWI began the HIPC initiative with the purpose of assisting poor countries that were sustaining potentially unmanageable amounts of debt.[63] The World Bank administers a trust fund (separate from its own resources) that is financed and administered by external donors and which allows the leveraging of poverty-reduction programs by providing expanding development collaboration, including technical assistance, advisory services, debt relief, and co-financing.[64] In response to harsh criticism of the qualifying criteria for the original HIPC, the IMF initiated and advanced a version of the Initiative in 1999.[65]

---

[62] *See* Daniel Cohen, *The HIPC Initiative: True and False Promises* 5 (OECD Dev. Centre, Working Paper No. 166, 2000). Furthermore, the G-7 Leaders have expressed doubt stating:

[N]ot all creditors have agreed to reduce their HIPC debts; the expected financing needs for the initiative have not been met, and as a result of weaker growth and export commodity prices, a number of countries could be at risk of not having sustainable debt loads at the Completion Point.

G-8 Sommet Kananaskis Summit, (Jun. 2002), http://ahibo.com/G8/en/aldeteg7.htm. The leaders encouraged the BWI to seek assistance from both regional and multilateral development institutions. *Id.* Furthermore, they requested the institutions seek additional assistance and availability from internal resources. *Id.* The leaders of the G-8 committed to contribute $1 billion to the initiative. *Id.*

[63] *See Debt Relief Under the Heavily Indebted Poor Countries (HIPC) Initiative, supra* note 24 (last visited Nov. 23, 2017); *see also* Eugenia McGill, *Poverty and Social Analysis of Trade Agreements: A More Coherent Approach?*, 27 B.C. INT'L & COMP. L. REV. 371, 380 (2004) (stating "The initiative was the result of a civil-society campaign for meaningful external debt relief to free up scarce financial resources to address HIV/AIDS and other social development needs.").

[64] *See* John R. Crook, *United States Supports G–7 Decisions to Reduce Debt Burden of Poor Countries, Including Those Affected by December 2004 Tsunamis*, 99 AM. J. INT'L. L. 500, 501 (2005); The United States has repeatedly encouraged other bilateral creditors to follow it on providing 100 percent loan forgiveness for MDB soft loans to the HIPCs. *Id.* Bonnie D. Jenkins, et. al., *International Institutions*, 37 INT'L LAW. 609 (2003).

[65] *See* Robin Goldberg, *Financing Developments and the Desperate Need for Debt Relief*, 17 N.Y.L. SCH. J. HUM. RTS. 969 (2001); Elizabeth Justice, *The African Union: Building A Dream to Facilitate Trade, Development, and Debt Relief*, 12 CURRENTS: INT'L TRADE L.J. 127, 130–31 (2003) (explaining that at its inception in 1996, only 5 countries qualified for the HIPC).

"In 2004, the World Bank stated: the enhanced HIPC initiative provides an opportunity to strengthen the economic prospects and poverty reduction efforts of its beneficiary countries."[66] Nevertheless, as of 2009, of the two trillion dollars owed by developing countries, about $250 billion is owed by nations that were given "low income" status.[67]

Critics claim that although the program has good intentions, the program is inadequate because it does not force debtor nations to adequately reduce poverty or provide basic health care and education for their citizens.[68] Irrespective of these shortcomings, budget cuts are often incurred in these areas to meet stringent demands for receiving debt relief.[69]

---

[66] *See* Mark J. Wolff, *Failure Of The International Monetary Fund & World Bank To Achieve Integral Development: A Critical Historical Assessment Of Bretton Woods Institutions' Policies, Structures & Governance*, 41 SYRACUSE J. INT'L L. & COM. 71 (2013). "When default becomes inescapable, the debts that governments cannot pay are almost always owed in foreign currency…an inability to stay current on payments on external debt causes deep economic trauma." Barry Herman, *Doing the Right Thing: Dealing with Developing Country Sovereign Debt*, 32 N.C.J. INT'L L. & COM. REG. 773, 775 (2007). During the time building up to the Monterrey Consensus, fifty-six countries had "arreares in their foreign debt payments or rescheduled their debt-servicing obligations…accounting for one-fifth of world's population, over one billion people, but less than six percent of world's gross product." *Id.* at 776. Middle-income countries such as Argentina, the Dominican Republic, and Iraq have also restructured debts they could no longer service. *See id.* "While IMF has usually assumed the role of international arbiter of how much relief, new financing, and policy reform a country needs to overcome its debt crisis, it has been widely accused of systematically underestimating the amount of relief needed." *Id.* at 779. There may be systematic bias for countries following IMF policy advice. *See id.*

[67] *See* David Ricksecker, *What is the HIPC Initiative?*, UNIV. OF IOWA CTR. FOR INT'L FIN. AND DEV. (Sept. 21, 2006), http://www.uiowa.edu/ifdebook/faq/faq_docs/HIPC.shtml (describing how without major debt reduction, poor income countries are trapped and stuck making endless interest payments on debts). Since inception of the initiative, Guyana is the only country that has successfully been removed from the list of heavily indebted poor countries. *See* Dijkstra, *supra* note 19, at 107. The problem with achieving sustainability through the HIPC is evident in its qualification methods: almost ten countries have not even reached the decision point and eight more have not reached completion. *See* Dijkstra, *supra* note 19.

[68] *See* A. Mechele Dickerson, *Insolvency Principles and the Odious Debt Doctrine: The Missing Link in the Debate*, 70 LAW & CONTEMP. PROBS. 53, 59 (2007).

[69] *See* UNITED NATIONS, *WORLD ECONOMIC SITUATIONS AND PROSPECTS* 77 (2009), http://www.un.org/en/development/desa/policy/wesp/wesp_archive/2009wesp.pdf. This

Currently, thirty-eight states are recognized as HIPC qualified.[70] The initiative provides low-interest loans and debt relief to reduce external debt payments and achieve levels sustainable for countries to reach "completion point."[71] Factors for considering whether a country is heavily indebted include "a nation's total outstanding debt relative to exports and GDP, as opposed to rations of debt service expenses to government revenues."[72] Further, qualification is conditional upon the governments' abilities to attain a range of economic management and performance targets as set and agreed upon with either the World Bank or the IMF.[73]

As the 'gatekeeper' for development assistance, the IMF requires HIPC countries to prepare and submit Poverty Reduction Strategy Papers (the "PRSPs") for approval, prior to receiving loans or debt relief.[74]

---

would require the reduction in poverty to mirror the release of government-subsidized programs. *Id.*

[70] *See Debt Relief Under The Heavily Indebted Poor Countries (HIPC) Initiative, supra* note 24. *See* Dickerson, *supra* note 68, at 59 (explaining that qualification requires eligible nations to have a current track record of satisfactory performance under a Poverty Reduction Strategy, an IMF program, or an interim PRS in place). An agreed plan must also be in place to clear any outstanding debts to foreign creditors. *Id.*

[71] *See Debt Relief Under The Heavily Indebted Poor Countries (HIPC) Initiative, supra* note 24 (describing the two-step process which countries must follow for HIPC Initiative assistance). The completion point is the second and final step where, upon completion, a country is allowed to receive its full debt relief committed at decision point. *See id.*

[72] *See* Charles Seavey, *The Anomalous Lack of an International Bankruptcy Court*, 24 BERKLEY J. INT'L L. 499, 504 (2006). These standards "penalize countries with: (i) low government tax revenues relative to exports or GDP; and/or (ii) high debt service relative to total outstanding debt." *Id.* at 517.

[73] *See* Ambrose, *supra* note 14, at 272 (stating "[Governments] with questionable credit-worthiness will only be considered eligible for grants, loans, or credits once the IMF has signaled its approval of the government's economic program.").

[74] *See Poverty Reduction Strategy Papers Fact Sheet*, INT'L MONETARY FUND (last updated Dec. 28, 2016), http://www.imf.org/external/np/prsp/prsp.asp#H. PRSP's are prepared by member countries (of the BWI's) and updated every three years. *Id.* PRSP's include annual progress reports, a description of macro and micro-economic policies and programs for promotion of growth and reduction of poverty. *Id.* Countries also provide interim PRSP's through the process of finalizing the fully-developed PRSP's. *See id.; see also* Lisa Philipps & Miranda Stewart, *Fiscal Transparency: Global Norms, Domestic Laws, and the Politics of Budgets*, 34 BROOK. J. INT'L L. 797, 817–21 (2009) (explaining several accounta-bility mechanisms, including PRSP's, that country donors have used to help strengthen and manage public finances and fiscal policy in aid-recipient countries). The PRSP's are

However, this type of loan-bargaining structure often ends up one-sided, placing the IMF in a totalitarian position regarding budget cuts in the debtor countries,[75] and thereby limiting availability of resources for public services.[76] While urging priority in repayment of debts, the IMF urges low-income countries to adopt potentially cataclysmic policies.[77]

---

meant to increase focus on poverty reduction while providing stronger collaboration between the country and the financing institutions. *Id.* More than sixty-six countries completed PRSP's between 2000 and March 2009. *Id.*

[75] *See* Dickerson, *supra* note 68, at 56. "Some members of the financial community . . . contend that IMF lending creates a moral-hazard problem…knowingly lending to repressive regimes who illegally divert the loan process or use the funds in ways that affirmatively harm the countries' citizens." *See id.* Contrary to the effects of its implementation, the PRSP's were supposed to grant governments greater influence in "tripartite" discussions for loan forgiveness and redevelopment. *See* MARC DARROW, BETWEEN LIGHT AND SHADOW: THE WORLD BANK, THE INTERNATIONAL MONETARY FUND, AND INTERNATIONAL HUMAN RIGHTS LAW 289 (2006). This allows for the IMF and World Bank policy makers to take advantage of the developing countries' weakness, diverting government attention regarding obligations from citizens to the institutions. *Id.; see* Fergus MacKay, *Universal Rights or a Universe unto Itself? Indigenous Peoples' Human Rights and the World Bank's Draft Operational Policy 4.10 on Indigenous Peoples,* 17 AM. U. INT'L L. REV. 527, 532–33 (2002); Ibrahim F. I. Shihata, *The World Bank and the IMF Relationship-Quo Vadis,* 35 INT'L LAW. 3549 (2001). However, it is been assessed most developing countries may not have the institutional capacity to conduct the necessary public consultations required for approval of a PRSP. *Id.; see* Rajesh Swaminathan, *Regulating Development: Structural Adjustment and the Case for National Enforcement of Economic and Social Rights,* 37 COLUM. J. TRANSNAT'L L. 161, 214 (1998). There are several operational issues regarding the interrelational aspects of these structural policies and individual human rights standards. *See id.*

[76] *See* Goldberg, *supra* note 65, at 970 (furthering insight into why countries participating in the HIPC run into problems even with their participation in the program). HIPC debtor countries usually apportion their domestic investments toward infrastructure, such as providing electrical power, paving roads, and telephone connections instead of spending money toward health and education. *See id.* This form of neoliberal economic ideology has proven detrimental to certain countries. *See* Anup Shah, *Structural Adjustment – A Major Cause of Poverty,* GLOBAL ISSUES, (Oct. 29, 2008), http://www.globalissues.org/print/article/3. Minimizing the role of the state, privatization, reduced protection of domestic industries, currency devaluation, increased interest rates, elimination of subsidies, reduction and removal of regulations to gain attraction from foreign investors are all parts if this ideology. *See id.* "Structural adjustments have…contributed to 'the greatest peacetime transfer of wealth from the periphery to the imperial center in history'…without much media attention." *Id.*

[77] *See* KUNIBERT RAFFER, DEBT MANAGEMENT FOR DEVELOPMENT: PROTECTION OF THE POOR AND THE MILLENIUM DEVELOPMENT GOALS 101 (2010).

121

Challenge of G-20

The Group of Twenty, otherwise known as G-20, is a group of finance ministers and central bank governors from countries across the world initially dedicated to discussing and coordinating policies related to the stabilization and regulation of global financial markets. But the group has recently broadened its agenda to include more general global economic governance issues.[78]

Established as a response to the financial crises of the late 1990s,[79] the G-20 consists of selected advanced and so-called "systemically significant" emerging economies.[80] The G-20 functions as an informal forum, allowing for discussion between the participating developed and developing countries as to the promotion of global economic stability and development.[81] The inaugural meeting of the G-20 took place in Berlin, Germany, on December 15-16, 1999.[82] Since then, the G-20 has held annual meetings, engaging in dialogue about key economic issues and implementing various initiatives and reforms.[83]

---

[78] *See* Haque & Burdescue, *supra* note 17, at 241 (explaining how leaders came to the Conference with the objective of establishing a framework for cooperation and assistance with alleviating poverty); *see also What is the G20?*, G-20 RESEARCH GROUP, http://www.g20.utoronto.ca/g20whatisit.html (last visited Aug. 21, 2017).

[79] *See G20 Leaders Statement: The Pittsburgh Summit*, G-20 RESEARCH GROUP (last visited Aug. 21, 2017), http://www.g20.utoronto.ca/2009/2009communique0925.html.

[80] *See What is the G20?*, *supra* note 78. The finance ministers and central bank governors hail from the European Union and the following nineteen countries: Argentina, Australia, Brazil, Canada, China, France, Germany, India, Indonesia, Italy, Japan, Mexico, Russia, Saudi Arabia, South Africa, Republic of Korea, Turkey, United Kingdom, and the United States. Former Canadian Finance Minister (later, Prime Minister) is credited with proposing the G-20. *See* John Ibbitson & Tara Perkins, *How Canada Made the G20 Happen*, THE GLOBE AND MAIL, (last updated Aug. 23, 2012, 3:26 PM), http://www.theglobeandmail.com/news/world/how-canada-made-the-g20-happen/article4322767/?page=all.

[81] *See What is the G20?*, *supra* note 78.

[82] *See id.*

[83] *See id.* The meetings are annual, but they are preceded by workshops, reports, case studies to provide ministers and governors with analysis and insight. *Id.* The 2011 G-20 summit meeting took place on November 3–4, 2011, in Cannes, France. *See 2011 G20 Cannes Summit*, G20 Research Group, http://www.g20.utoronto.ca/summits/2011cannes.html (last visited Aug. 21, 2017).

Creation of the G-20 was premised in part on remedying the limited participation of key emerging developing economies in global economic discussion and governance.[84] Other forums discussing world economic issues preceded the G-20, and these "showed the potential benefits of a regular international consultative forum embracing the emerging-market countries."[85] Building on these predecessors, the hand-picked G-20 members enabled a regular dialogue with a constant set of partners.[86]

Reflecting the broad representation of the G-20, its member countries represent around ninety percent of global national product, eighty percent of world trade, and two-thirds of the world population.[87] However, critics of the G-20 mention that it is essentially a self-appointed, elite group, and point to its corresponding lack of inclusiveness, accountability and, most importantly, political legitimacy.[88]

Because of the informal nature of the G-20, members can make comments, recommendations, and measures to be adopted.[89] There are no

---

[84] See G20 Leaders Statement: The Pittsburgh Summit, supra note 79 (noting that prior to the establishment of the G-20, key emerging market countries were not adequately included in global economic discussion and governance).

[85] Global Economic Forum G-20, GOVERNMENT OF THE CZECH REPUBLIC (Mar. 27, 2009) https://www.vlada.cz/en/media-centrum/aktualne/global-economic-forum-g-20-will-be-held-on-the-2nd-april-in-london-55305/. Before the G-20 was created, there was a G-22, G-7, and even a G-33. Id. These groups of leaders made proposals to deal with world economic issues. Id. The G-7 was established in 1976, comprised of major industrial economies including "Canada, France, Germany, Italy, Japan . . . , the United Kingdom and the United States of America." OECD Glossary of Statistical Terms, OECD, https://stats.oecd.org/glossary/detail.asp?ID=6806 (last visited Aug. 21, 2017). The G-7 also allows for discussion of current economic issues, but the discussion is geared toward the interests of the seven countries. Id. The G-20, in contrast, reflects the diverse interests of the industrial and emerging-market economies. See Global Economic Forum G-20, supra note 85.

[86] See id.

[87] See id.

[88] See Ulf Sverdrup and Joachim Nahem, The G20: Inclusivity and Legitimacy, FEDERAL ACADEMY FOR SECURITY POLICY (2017) https://www.baks.bund.de/sites/baks010/files/working_paper_2017_12.pdf .

[89] See Global Economic Forum G-20, supra note 85. Participation in the G-20 meetings is limited to the members. Sverdrup and Nahem, supra note 88. The limit is linked to ensuring the "effectiveness and continuity of [the G–20's] activity. Chris Brummer, Soft Law

formal votes or resolutions.[90] Instead, "[e]very G-20 member has one 'voice' with which it can take an active part in G-20 activity."[91] There is no permanent staff. The chair, selected from a different regional group of countries, rotates on an annual basis.[92] The chair is part of a three-member management "Troika" of chairs.[93]

Financial ministers and central bank governors are not the only attendees at G-20 meeting.[94] Also present at the meetings are important representatives of the BWI, namely the Managing Director of the IMF, the President of the World Bank, and the chairs of the International Monetary and Financing Committee and Development Committee of the IMF and World Bank.[95] This participation attempts to ensure that the G-20 process is "well integrated" with the activities of the BWI.[96]

Reform of the BWI has, indeed, been on the agenda of more than one G-20 meeting.[97] Acknowledging the "vital role the [BWI] should play in promoting macroeconomic and financial stability, economic growth, and poverty reduction,"[98] the G-20 concentrated in great part on gov-

and the Global Financial System 320 (CAMBRIDGE UNIVERSITY PRESS, Sep 29, 2015). Although the meetings are not open to the public, the public has access to discussions via a "communiqué" which the G–20 publishes after each meeting. *See e.g. G–20 Publications,* G–20,
http://www.bundesfinanzministerium.de/Content/DE/Standardartikel/Themen/Schlaglic hter/G20-2016/g20-communique.pdf?__blob=publicationFile&v=10 (last visited Nov. 23, 2017) (providing record of communiqués).

[90] Brummer, *supra* note 89, at 73. There are no voting shares attached to the voting member, and voting power is not governed by the member's economic status. *See id.* at 65.

[91] Brummer, *supra* note 89, at 74. "To this extent, the influence a country can exert is shaped decisively by its commitment." *See id.* at 73.

[92] *See What is the G20?, supra* note 78 (stating the 2011 Chair is France). Mexico will chair the G20 in 2012. *See id.* Starting in 2011, G–20 summits will be held annually. *See id.*

[93] Brummer, *supra* note 89, at 73.

[94] *See id.* at 72.

[95] *See id.* at 107 (stating these participate on an ex–officio basis.).

[96] *See What is the G20?, supra* note 78. The G–20 also collaborates with the Financial Stability Board and the Basel Committee on Banking Supervision. *See Financial Stability Board and International Standards,* CIGI (Jun. 1, 2010),
https://www.cigionline.org/sites/default/files/g20_no_1_2.pdf.

[97] *See G-20 Statement on Reforming Bretton Woods Institutions,* G20 RESEARCH GROUP (Oct. 16, 2005), http://www.g20.utoronto.ca/2005/2005bwi.html.

[98] *Id.*

ernance reforms.[99] Recognizing the evolution of the global economy since the inception of the BWI,[100] the G-20's statement emphasized the need to have the governance structure of the BWI "reflect such changes in economic weight" with respect to both quotas and representation.[101]

The 2005 Statement also addressed management reforms.[102] The Statement suggested that the BWI work to enhance their "institutional effectiveness" advising that selection of senior management should be premised on merit and to allow for broad representation of all member countries.[103] The G-20 also drew attention to lending practices, advising the BWI's to "continue improving their lending frameworks," and to take measures to meet their members' financial needs.[104]

---

[99] *See id.* The G-20 also called for reinforcement of the cooperation between the BWI and discussed their separate responsibilities. *See id.* The G-20 emphasized that the IMF should focus on macroeconomic and financial stability, both nationally and internationally, on the surveillance of the global economy, and on strengthening crisis prevention. *G-20 Statements on Reforming Bretton Woods Institution, supra* note 97. As to the World Bank, the G-20 advised that its focus on development "sharpening its financial and technical assistance roles for both least–developed countries and emerging markets." *See id. See also Communiqué,* G20 RESEARCH GROUP (Oct. 16, 2005), http://www.g20.utoronto.ca/2005/2005communique.html (reiterating support for reformation of the BWI and drawing attention to the importance of improving the governance, management, and operational strategies of the BWI).

[100] *G-20 Statement on Reforming the Bretton Woods Institution, supra* note 97 (stating specifically, the growth in emerging markets and "deepened integration in industrialized countries.")

[101] *See id.*

[102] *See id.*

[103] *See id.*

[104] *See id.* The 2006 G-20 meeting renewed discussion regarding the reform of the BWI. *See Communiqué,* G-20 RESEAWRCH GROUP (Nov. 19, 2006), http://www.g20.utoronto.ca/2006/2006communique.html (last visited Apr. 10, 2017). At the meeting, members discussed the formula of a quota formula and how to implement it. *Id.* The members also agreed to further consider issues relating to IMF surveillance, the IMF's role in emerging market economies, and its role in low–income countries, as well as collaboration between the BWI. *Id.* The members called for the modernization and strengthening of IMF surveillance to "meet the demands of globalisation." *Id.* Suggesting a possible weakness in the area of surveillance, the G-20 addressed the strengthening of IMF surveillance as recently as 2011, noting G-20 agreement on the need to further strengthen the effectiveness and coherence of bilateral and multilateral IMF surveillance. *See* Final Communiqué, Meeting of G20 Finance Ministers and Central Bank Governors in Wash. D.C. (Apr. 15, 2011),

The 2008 financial crisis gave the G-20 forum a new dimension and prompted the G-20 to call for continued BWI reform.[105] By 2004, Canadian Prime Minister Paul Martin wanted the G-20 to not only be a forum for finance ministers and central bank governors, but also one for the leaders of the governments.[106]

Martin's goal came to fruition as a result of the 2008 financial crisis, when then-president George W. Bush decided to convene a meeting of world leaders to deal with the crisis.[107] The Bush administration gathered the world leaders by turning to the G-20 countries.[108] The result was the G-20 Summit, which convened on November 15, 2008, and featured a gathering of both finance ministers and political leaders.[109]

Notwithstanding its lack of inclusiveness (and legitimacy), the Washington, D.C. summit has been billed by some as the "Bretton Woods 2" meeting for its emphasis on reform of the BWI.[110] After the Summit, the G-20 issued a declaration setting forth reforms to be implemented in response to the ongoing financial crisis.[111] The G-20 noted five categories of reform and characterized the measures to be taken in each category as either "immediate" or "medium term."[112]

Reform of international financial institutions was one such category.[113] Recognizing the plight of developing economies as to financing, the G-

---

http://www.g20.utoronto.ca/2011/2011-finance-110415-en.html.

[105] *See* Ibbitson & Perkins, *supra* note 80.

[106] *See id.*

[107] *See id.*

[108] *See id.*

[109] *See id.* Since then, the leaders of the G-20 nations have held summits semi-annually or annually. *See* Ibbitson & Perkins, *supra* note 80. Summits were held in London and Pittsburg in 2009. *See id.* Summits were also held in Toronto in 2010. *See id.*

[110] *See G20 Heads of State Meeting 15th November 2008: Summary and Analysis of Washington Meeting*, BRETTON WOODS PROJECT (Nov. 17, 2008), http://www.brettonwoodsproject.org/2008/11/art-562975/.

[111] *See Declaration of the Summit on Financial Markets and the World Economy*, G20 RESEARCH GROUP (Nov. 15, 2008), http://www.g20.utoronto.ca/2008/2008declaration1115.html.

[112] *Declaration of the Summit on Financial Markets and the World Economy, supra* note 111.

[113] *See id.* The IMF and World Bank were the focus of this category of reform. *Id.* The other categories of reform were: strengthening transparency and accountability; enhanc-

20 expressed approval of the IMF's new short-term liquidity facility and urged the "ongoing review of its instruments and facilities to ensure flexibility."[114] As to the World Bank, the G-20 encouraged full-capacity use of its development agenda, approving the "introduction of new facilities by the World Bank in the areas of infrastructure and trade finance."[115] The G-20 expressed its intent to act to "[e]nsure that the [BWI's] ... have sufficient resources to continue playing their role in overcoming the crisis."[116]

The November declaration emphasized the state of developing and emerging economies in urging BWI reform.[117] The G-20 tied BWI reform to these countries, noting its commitment to the BWI' reform "so that they can more adequately reflect changing economic weights in the world economy."[118] It called for International Financial Institutions to review and adapt their lending instruments to meet their members' needs, and also called for consideration of ways to "restore emerging and developing countries' access to credit and resume private capital flows which are critical for sustainable growth and development, including ongoing infrastructure investment."[119]

The G-20 once again addressed the issue of surveillance, noting that the IMF should conduct "vigorous and even-handed surveillance reviews of all countries."[120] Elaborating on another weakness in IMF

---

ing sound regulation; promoting integrity in financial markets; and reinforcing international cooperation. *Id.* The proposed reforms were separated into five categories: (1) strengthening transparency and accountability; (2) enhancing sound regulation; (3) promoting integrity in financial markets; (4) reinforcing international cooperation; (5) reforming international financial institutions. *See Declaration of the Summit on Financial Markets and the World Economy, supra* note 111.

[114] *See id.*

[115] *See id.*

[116] *See id.*

[117] *See id.*

[118] *See id.* The G20 also noted that the FSF should expand to a broad membership of emerging economies. *See Declaration of the Summit on Financial Markets and the World Economy, supra* note 111.

[119] *See id.*

[120] *Declaration of the Summit on Financial Markets and the World Economy, supra* note 111.

operations, the G-20 stated the BWI's role in providing macro-financial policy advice would be strengthened if it gave "greater attention to the financial sectors of all countries and better integrated the reviews with the joint IMF/World Bank financial sector assessment programs."[121]

IMF operations were once again a source of discussion during the April 2009 G-20 Summit, which occurred in London.[122] In a declaration issued after the Summit, G-20 leaders noted the continued need to reinforce international financial institutions, "particularly the IMF."[123]

To that end, the G-20 pledged to make available $850 billion in resources through the global financial institutions "to support growth in emerging market and developing countries by helping to finance counter-cyclical spending, bank recapitalization, infrastructure, trade finance, balance of payments support, debt rollover, and social support."[124] The G-20 agreed to increase the resources available to the IMF

---

[121] *See id.* The G-20 also addressed crisis response, emphasizing the need for the IMF to collaborate with the FSF and other bodies in an effort to "better identify vulnerabilities, anticipate potential stresses, and act swiftly to play a key role in crisis response." *See id.* Part of the action plan was for the IMF, in conjunction with the expanded FSF and other regulators and bodies, to develop recommendations to "mitigate pro–cyclicality, including the review of how valuation and leverage, bank capital, executive compensation, and provisioning practices may exacerbate cyclical trends." *See id.*

[122] *See Global Plan for Recovery and Reform*, G20 RESEARCH GROUP (Apr. 2, 2009), http://www.g20.utoronto.ca/2009/2009communique0402.html.

[123] *Id.*

[124] *Id.* Counter-cyclical spending is a fiscal policy characterized by an increase in government expenditures that is meant to jumpstart economic recovery. *See* Martin Khor, *Reality Behind the Hype of G20 Summit*, THIRD WORLD NETWORK (Apr. 6, 2009), http://www.twn.my/title2/resurgence/2009/224/cover1.htm. "Programs that automatically expand fiscal policy during recessions and contract it during booms– are one form of countercyclical fiscal policy. *See* David N. Weil, *Fiscal Policy*, THE CONCISE ENCYCLOPEDIA OF ECON. (last visited Nov. 23, 2017), http://www.econlib.org/library/Enc/FiscalPolicy.html. Additionally, bank recapitalization refers to the restructuring of a troubled bank with the assistance of a deposit insurance fund. *See Business Definition for: Recapitalization*, ALL BUSSINESS (last visited Nov. 23, 2017), http://www.allbusiness.com/glossaries/recapitalization/4954442-1.html. Debt rollover refers to the rolling over of existing debt into new debt when the existing debt is about to mature. *See Rollover Risk*, INVESTOPEDIA (last visited Nov. 23, 2017), http://www.investopedia.com/terms/r/rollover-risk.asp#axzz1Zls25wls. The IMF defines balance of payments as a:

through immediate financing of $250 billion from members, and announced its "support for a substantial increase in lending of at least $100 billion by the Multilateral Development Banks," specifically to low income countries.[125] Many of these same topics were revisited and reiterated at the November 2011 summit meeting in Cannes, France.

statistical statement that systematically summarizes, for a specific time period, the economic transactions of an economy with the rest of the world. Transactions, for the most part between residents and nonresidents, consist of those involving goods, services, and income; those involving financial claims on, and liabilities to, the rest of the world; and those (such as gifts) classified as transfers, which involve offsetting entries to balance—in an accounting sense—one-sided transactions.
Balance of Payment Manual, INTERNATIONAL MONETARY FUND (last visited Nov. 23, 2017), http://www.imf.org/external/np/sta/bop/bopman.pdf.
[125] *Global Plan for Recovery and Reform, supra* note 122.

5

CONCLUSION

O ver more than six decades, the United States and key European-Union nation-states have dominated the Bretton Woods Institutions by controlling the International Monetary Fund and World Bank.

In recent decades, they have forced governments of developing countries to impose neoliberal policies on their own societies, with the false claim that such neoliberal policies were necessary to achieve the earlier Millennium Development Goals and the more recent Sustainable Development Goals.[1] Yet, in key cases, the governments of major developed countries have hypocritically rejected those very same neoliberal policies for their own countries.

For example, within the United States in 2008, the two mortgage giants known as the Federal National Mortgage Association ("Fannie Mae") and the Federal Home Loan Mortgage Corporation ("Freddie Mac") suffered deep financial losses and investors lost confidence in them. In response and contrary to neoliberal doctrines, the United States government, at the behest of the Federal Reserve, intervened in the 'free market' by passing legislation to have the government bailout both institutions (at taxpayers' expense) and take them over.[2]

---

[1]. *See supra* Chapter I note 21 and accompanying text.
[2] *See Federal National Mortgage Association Fannie Mae*, N.Y. TIMES (last updated Oct. 12, 2011),
http://topics.nytimes.com/top/news/business/companies/fannie_mae/index.html?inline=n

In addition, amidst the same economic recession and shortly after the fall of Lehman Brothers,[3] the American International Group ("AIG") suffered a liquidity crisis of financially epic proportions and was on the brink of bankruptcy. As a result, in September 2008 its credit ratings were downgraded to A- from AA-.[4] Fearing catastrophic consequences from an AIG bankruptcy, the Federal Reserve Board announced on September 16 that it would authorize the Federal Reserve Bank of New York to lend up to $85 billion to AIG – again, contrary to neoliberal policies.[5]

Yet again in 2008, the United States automotive industry faced a major financial downturn, partially due to a substantial increase in fuel pric-

---

yt-org; *Freddie Mac*, N.Y. TIMES (last updated Sept. 2, 2011), http://topics.nytimes.com/top/news/business/companies/freddie_mac/index.html?inline=nyt-org; Charles Duhigg, *As Crisis Grew, A Few Options Shrank to One*, N.Y. TIMES, Sept. 7, 2008, http://www.nytimes.com/2008/09/08/business/08takeover.html?_r=2&hp=&pagewanted=all&oref=slogin) (stating "[t]he downfall of Fannie and Freddie stems from a series of miscalculations and deferred decisions, both by their executives and government officials, according to company insiders, regulators, auditors and outside analysts.").

[3] *See* John Cassidy, *Anatomy of a Meltdown: Ben Bernanke and the Financial Crisis*, THE NEW YORKER (Dec. 1, 2008), http://www.newyorker.com/reporting/2008/12/01/081201fa_fact_cassidy?currentPage=all; Sam Mamudi, *Lehman Folds with Record $613 Billion Debt*, MARKETWATCH (Sept 15, 2008, 10:11 AM), http://www.marketwatch.com/story/lehman-folds-with-record-613-billion-debt?siteid=rss. Lehman Brothers, a Wall Street investment bank, filed for bankruptcy protection in 2008. *Id.* The bankruptcy was the largest in history, with a total of $613 billion in debt against $639 billion in assets. *Id.* The bankruptcy effectively ended the company's 158-year existence. *Id.*

[4] *See* William Greider, *The AIG Bailout Scandal*, THE NATION (Aug. 6, 2010), http://www.thenation.com/article/153929/aig-bailout-scandal?page=full; *see also* Jim Puzzanghera, *AIG Bailout is 'Poisonous'; Taxpayers Risk 'Severe Losses,' Panel Says*, L.A. TIMES (June 11, 2010), http://articles.latimes.com/2010/jun/11/business/la-fi-aig-bailout-20100611 (referring to the bailout as a $182-billion bailout and noting the lack of clarity as to whether taxpayers ever will be fully repaid).

[5] Press Release, Board of Governors of the Federal Reserve System (Sept. 16, 2008), http://www.federalreserve.gov/newsevents/press/other/20080916a.htm; Pam Selvarajah, *VIII. The AIG Bailout and AIG's Prospects for Repaying Government Loans*, 29 REV. BANKING & FIN. L. 363, 364 (2010) (noting that the loan carried a twenty-four-month term).

es.[6] And again, the United States government took an action that abandoned the neoliberal policies imposed on developing countries. With taxpayer dollars, the United States government gave large government bailouts to General Motors and Chrysler, in order to rescue them from their financial crisis. At the same time, it gave the Ford Motor Company an open credit-line from the Federal Reserve Bank.[7]

However, in 2009, due to poor management and business practices, General Motors and Chrysler were still required to file for Chapter 11 Bankruptcy.[8] After that bankruptcy, the Obama Administration agreed to commit another $30 billion to General Motors, on top of the $19.4 billion already given by the United States before the bankruptcy. In return, the United States took a 60% equity stake in the new General Motors Company.[9] Such actions, of course, were completely contrary to neoliberal policies.

The United States has not been the only developed country to institute such hypocritical policies. The IMF, dominated by European economies, bailed out Greece, Ireland, Portugal, and Cyprus.[10] Additionally,

---

[6] *See Gas Prices Put Detroit Big Three in Crisis Mode,* ASSOCIATED PRESS (June 1, 2008), http://www.msnbc.msn.com/id/24896359/ns/business-autos/t/gas-prices-put-detroit-big-three-crisis-mode/#.TsBwSMPNltM.

[7] *See* David Shepardson, *Rattner Applauds Auto Bailouts' 'Happy Ending',* THE DETROIT NEWS (Nov. 1, 2011), http://detnews.com/article/20111101/AUTO01/111010321/Rattner-applauds-auto-bailouts%E2%80%99-%E2%80%98happy-ending%E2%80%99 (noting that the Treasury extended Chrysler a $12.5 billion bailout, $11.3 billion of which has been recovered, and extended General Motors a $49.5 billion bailout, of which $23.2 billion has been recovered). "At current trading prices, the Treasury would lose more than $13 billion on its GM bailout." *Id.*

[8] *See* David Welch, *GM Files for Bankruptcy* BLOOMBERG (Jun. 1 2009), https://www.bloomberg.com/news/articles/2009-06-01/gm-files-for-bankruptcybusinessweek-business-news-stock-market-and-financial-advice.

[9] Isidore, Chris, *GM to Head Into Bankruptcy,* CNN MONEY (June 1, 2009), http://money.cnn.com/2009/05/31/news/companies/gm_bankruptcy_looms/index.htm?postversion=2009053112.

[10] *See The IMF and the Crises in Greece, Ireland, and Portugal,* INDEPENDENT EVALUATION OFFICE OF THE INTERNATIONAL MONETARY FUND (2016), http://www.ieo-imf.org/ieo/pages/CompletedEvaluation267.aspx (providing a comprehensive report card on the European debt crisis that impacted the continent from 2010 to 2013, the responses of the IMF to mitigate the crisis at that time, and the outcome and recommendations to

the European Union bailed out of some of its largest banks.[11] The recommendation to do so came directly from the IMF's managing director, Christine Lagarde.[12] Once, again, such actions contradicted neoliberal policies.

In agreement with that recommendation, the first major European bank bailout occurred in 2011, when the governments of both France and Belgium pledged to participate in a rescue plan for their banking giant Dexia.[13] The plan was to place Dexia's "toxic assets, including Greek and other peripheral euro-zone government bonds" into a government-supported "bad-bank."[14] Bank of France Governor and G20 member, Christian Noyer, stated: "[W]e will loan Dexia as much as it needs."[15]

---

better prepare the institution for future crises). From 2010 to 2013, the IMF provided fifty-eight billion euros to Greece, over twenty-two billion euros to Ireland, twenty-six billion euros to Portugal and one billion euros to Cyprus. *Id.* at 4. The report is critical of the IMF's Eurocentric tendencies that led to more favorable deals for European countries than would be the norm for other members of the institution. *Id.* The report argues that the European debt crisis started as a result of a "sudden stop" of foreign investment. *Id.* The report blames the speed at which the crisis took over the Euro zone on the indiscipline of some Euro zone member states. *Id.* The report argues that Greece received preferential treatment at the IMF because the institution did not require debt restructuring before providing loans. *Id.* The Managing Director made the decision to provide the loans without the necessary debt restructuring due to political pressures from European leaders. *Id.* As a result, the report's main recommendation is that the IMF develop procedures to reduce the involvement of political actors in the decision-making process of the institution. *Id.*

[11] Heather Stewart, Jill Treanor & Dominic Rushe, *IMF Chief Tells Europe: You Must Bail Out the Banks Again*, THE GUARDIAN (Sept 22, 2011), http://www.guardian.co.uk/world/2011/sep/22/imf-chief-europe-bail-out-banks.

[12] *Id.* (discussing Lagarde's call for action).

[13] Philip Blenkinsop & Robert-Jan Bartunek, *Dexia Bailout Set as Wider Bank Rescue Mulled*, REUTERS (Oct. 9, 2011), http://www.reuters.com/article/2011/10/09/us-dexia-idUSTRE7962XE20111009. Dexia used short-term funding to finance long-term lending, and had difficulty obtaining credit as the European debt crisis worsened. *Id.*

[14] John O'Donnell & Illona Wissenbach, *EU Preparing Bank Rescues Amid Greece Doubts*, REUTERS (Oct. 4, 2011), http://www.reuters.com/article/2011/10/04/us-eurozone-idUSTRE79211720111004.

[15] Alexandria Sage, *France's Noyer Says Will Ensure Dexia Liquidity*, REUTERS (Oct. 5, 2011), http://www.reuters.com/article/2011/10/05/france-dexia-noyer-idUSP6E7KC01N20111005.

Since developed countries have repeatedly abandoned neoliberal policies to protect their own economies, the BWI now also needs to recognize the harm done to developing countries by forcing neoliberal policies on them. In turn, there is urgent need for two major reforms of the BWI.

- The first urgently needed reform is for member states to *put individuals in power who will look out for the betterment of developing countries*.

- The second urgently needed reform is for member states to *establish an independent United Nations committee responsible for representing developing nations in negotiating loans and loan conditions, as well as in regulating uniformity with regard to tax issues of developing countries*.

Regarding the first proposed major reform of individuals in power, a hopeful event was when the former Finance Minister of France Ms. Christine Lagarde[16] took over the top post at the IMF. She did so in the midst of global economic turmoil, and after edging out the Bank of Mexico's governor Agustin Carstens,[17] With a promise to bring "re-

---

[16] *See Profile: Christine Lagarde, 'rock star' head of the IMF*, BBC (last visited Nov. 23, 2017) http://www.bbc.com/news/business-13452436 (providing a detailed summary of the IMF director's biography); *Christine Lagarde Biographical Information*, INTERNATIONAL MONETARY FUND, (last visited Nov. 23, 2017) https://www.imf.org/external/np/omd/bios/cl.htm; John Henley (outlining the responsibilities of the IMF director and the goals she aims during her tenure), *Christine Lagarde, IMF chief with a key role in the Greek debt talks – profile*, theguardian.com (last visited May 29, 2017) https://www.theguardian.com/world/2015/jun/26/profile-christine-lagarde-imf-greek-crisis-negotiations (providing a detailed analysis of the IMF Director's role and actions during the Greek debt crisis). Christine Lagarde was France's finance minister before taking over as head of the IMF. *Profile, supra.* During her time as head of the IMF she has received praise for her actions during the European debt crisis, especially her decision to provide loans to European countries with favorable terms attached to the loan guarantees. *See id.* However, some of her critics have complaint of the continued European dominance at the IMF that continues under her leadership. *See id.* In December 2016 she was convicted of negligence involving her decision to assist a French tycoon during her time as finance minster. *Profile, supra.*

[17] *Press Release No. 11/259, IMF Executive Board Selects Christine Lagarde as Managing Director*, INT'L MONETARY FUND, (Jan. 28, 2011), http://www.imf.org/external/np/sec/pr/2011/pr11259.htm.

form" to the IMF, Ms. Lagarde won the support of a several key economic powers. including China, Russia, and the United States.[18] As IMF Managing Director, she has been trying to move toward a more balanced approach (to the degree that she can).

Thus far, Ms. Lagarde's most prominent contribution to reform has been to increase the presence of emerging economies at the IMF. Yet several emerging market leaders voiced concern over the election of yet another European to head the IMF, something that has not changed since its inception in 1944.[19] Ms. Lagarde offset such complaints by her assurance that, under her leadership, the interests of emerging markets would be represented.[20]

To show her commitment, Ms. Lagarde created a fourth deputy managing director position, and appointed Chinese economist Zhu Min to the position. Cornell University Professor Eswar S. Prassar hailed the move as a "grand bargain," in that Europeans were able to keep control of the top job at the IMF while emerging markets were able to gain more of a voice with the appointment.[21]

In regard to the second proposed major reform, namely the establishment of an independent UN committee to increase the voice of developing countries, the present ad-hoc group of experts on international cooperation in tax matters could be converted into a subsidiary body of the United Nations Economic and Social Council[22] ("ECOSOC"[23]).

---

[18] *See US Backs Christine Lagarde as Next Head of IMF*, THE TELEGRAPH (June 28, 2011), http://www.telegraph.co.uk/news/worldnews/dominique-strauss-kahn/8603421/US-backs-Christine-Lagarde-as-next-head-of-IMF.html.

[19] *See* Liz Alderman, *France's, Lagarde, Named New Head of I.M.F.*, N.Y. TIMES (June 28, 2011), http://www.nytimes.com/2011/06/29/business/global/29fund.html.

[20] *See* Liz Alderman & Keith Bradsher, *Emerging Nations Warm to Lagarde for I.M.F. Role*, N.Y. TIMES (June 8, 2001),

http://www.nytimes.com/2011/06/08/business/global/08fund.html? pagewanted=all.

[21] Binyamin Appelbaum, *U.S. and Chinese Officials Named to I.M.F. Posts*, N.Y. TIMES (July 12, 2011), http://www.nytimes.com/2011/07/13/business/us-and-chinese-officials-named-to-imf-posts.html.

[22] *See Committee of Experts on International Cooperation in Tax Matters*, Financing for Development http://www.un.org/esa/ffd/tax/ (last visited Nov. 23, 2017). ECOSOC was estab-

This is not the first time that scholars have pointed out the need for a United Nations committee of experts to strengthen the voice of developing countries.[24] For example, a representative of Azerbaijan (a developing country) had earlier noted that one of the main challenges facing developing countries is tax evasion.[25] Yet, while each country is ultimately responsible for its tax system, neoliberal policies promoted by the BWI have nonetheless fostered loopholes within developing countries' tax systems.[26]

---

lished under the authority of the United Nations charter "as the principal organ to coordinate economic, social, and related work of the 14 UN specialized agencies, functional commissions and five regional commissions." *Background Information: Information About the Council,* UN ECONOMIC AND SOCIAL COUNCIL (last visited Nov. 23, 2017), http://www.un.org/en/ecosoc/about/index.shtml; *see also* U.N. Charter art. 61-72. "ECOSOC serves as the central forum for discussing international economic and social issues, and for formulating policy recommendations addressed to Member States and the United Nations system." *See id.*

[23] Press Release, ECOSOC, Proposals to Strengthen Voice of Developing Countries and Ensure Smooth Transition to Development Debated in Economic and Social Council (July 21, 2004), http://www.un.org/News/Press/docs/2004/ecosoc6133.doc.htm.

[24] *See* Marcelo Suarez Salvia, *Statement on Behalf of the Group of 77 and China,* G77.ORG (July 27, 2011) http://www.g77.org/statement/getstatement.php?id=110727C.

[25] *See Press Release, ECOSOC, Proposals to Strengthen Voice of Developing Countries and Ensure Smooth Transition to Development Debated in Economic and Social Council, supra* note 23.

[26] *See, e.g.,* CHRISTIAN AID, DEATH AND TAXES: THE TRUE TOLL OF TAX DODGING 8 (May 2008), http://www.christianaid.org.uk/images/deathandtaxes.pdf. A transfer price is the price that affiliated companies pay each other for an exchange of goods and services. *Id.* For the transaction to be legitimate, the transfer price should be what an arm's-length principle should pay in an open-market. *Id.* However, many prices are distorted in order to allow a corporation to shift income and minimize tax liability. *Id.* A report from Christian Aid estimates that the loss of corporate taxes to developing countries is approximately 160 billion dollars a year due to the practice of transfer pricing along with false invoicing. *Id.* at 2. Between 2000 and 2015, it is estimated that a total of 2.5 trillion dollars will have been lost due to these two practices. *Id.* Raising tax revenue is critical to developing countries specifically because it can help end a country's reliance on global aid. Rushanara Ali, *Tax Avoidance Hurts Both Britain and Developing Countries,* LABOURLIST (Feb. 9, 2013 12:59 PM), http://labourlist.org/2013/02/tax-avoidance-hurts-both-britain-and-developing-countries/. The 160 billion dollars per year that is lost to transfer pricing greatly exceeds the amount of aid that these countries receive. *Id.* The practice of transfer pricing affects developing countries most because these countries typically lack the necessary information from the companies involved to challenge this practice; EUROPEAN COMMISSION, TRANSFER PRICING AND DEVELOPING COUNTRIES 8 http://ec.europa.eu/europeaid/what/economic-support/documents/transfer-pricing-

These two above noted two and urgently needed reforms have been recommended by the G7 and the Monterrey Consensus. In addition, that urgency was reaffirmed at the International Conference on Financing for Development at Doha. But, so far, no action has been taken to allow a body of the United Nations any governing oversight over the economic power of the BWI.

Further, in response to the 2008 global economic turmoil,[27] various heads of state at the 2009 Conference on World Financial and Economic Crisis stressed the need for transparency with respect to financial markets.[28] To reduce the likelihood of future crises, they argued that all risks need to be disclosed to market participants.[29] They also recommended strengthening "transparency by originators and issuers of securitized products about the underwriting standards for, and the results of due diligence on, the underlying assets" – in order to prevent market participants from being misled.[30]

Improved financial-market transparency needs to include items that were most problematic during the financial crisis: undisclosed risks, off-the-balance-sheet items, and judgments and estimates.[31] Greater transparency can be accomplished by improving the presentation of financial statements and going "beyond required disclosures to provide

---

study_en.pdf. In addition, most developing countries lack legislation or regulations that specifically deal with the issue of transfer pricing. *Id.* at 22.

[27] Bulent Gokay, *The 2008 World Economic Crisis: Global Shifts and Faultlines*, GLOBAL RESEARCH (Feb. 15, 2009), http://www.globalresearch.ca/the-2008-world-economic-crisis-global-shifts-and-faultlines/12283.

[28] Outcome of the Conference on the World Financial and Economic Crisis and Its Impact on Development, G.A. Res. 63/303, ¶ 37, U.N. Doc. A/RES/63/303 (July 13, 2009), http://www.un.org/ga/search/view_doc.asp?symbol=A/RES/63/303&Lang=E.

[29] *See* Noel Sacasa, Preventing Future Crises, FINANCE & DEVELOPMENT, 11 (2008), https://www.imf.org/external/pubs/ft/fandd/2008/12/pdf/fd1208.pdf.

[30] *Id.* at 14.

[31] *See* Monica Singh, *More Transparent Financial Reporting Disclosures Needed to Boost Investor Trust*, CFA INSTITUTE (July 29, 2013), http://blogs.cfainstitute.org/marketintegrity/2013/07/29/more-transparent-financial-reporting-disclosures-needed-to-boost-investor-trust/.

investors with a complete understanding of the underlying economic effects of transactions and account balances."[32]

On October 21, 2013, the Committee of Experts on International Cooperation in Tax Matters met in Geneva for their Ninth Session.[33] The Committee finalized an amendment to a 2001 commentary recommending that countries follow the OECD Transfer Pricing Guidelines for Multinational Enterprises and Tax Administrations (the "OECD Transfer Pricing Guidelines").[34] The amendment states that the OECD Transfer Pricing Guidelines should be used with regard to transfer-pricing of goods, technology, trademarks and services between enterprises not made at arm's-length.[35]

That same Ninth Session also created a Subcommittee on Base Erosion and Profit Shifting.[36] Among its concerns, this Subcommittee recommended the following:

---

[32] *Id.*

[33] *See Ninth Session of the Committee of Experts on International Cooperation in Tax Matters,* FINANCING FOR DEVELOPMENT (March 8, 2014), http://www.un.org/esa/ffd/tax/ninthsession/index.htm.

[34] *See* Comm. of Experts on Int'l Cooperation in Tax Matters, Note by the Secretariat, Oct. 21-5, 2013, U.N. Doc. E/C.18/2013/4 (Aug. 9, 2013), http://www.un.org/ga/search/view_doc.asp?symbol=E/2013/45&Lang=E

[35] *Id.* An arm's length transaction is one in which the price and other conditions of the transaction are determined by the market forces. *See Transfer Pricing Guidelines for Multinational Enterprises and Tax Administration,* OECD (July 2010), http://www.oecd.org/corporate/mne/1922428.pdf. An arm's length transaction is a transaction that occurs in an open market between unrelated taxpayers. Joseph Andrus, *Transfer Pricing and the Arm's Length Principle,* WORLD COMMERCE REVIEW 28 (June 2012), http://www.worldcommercereview.com/publications/article_pdf/625. This principle is the basis for transfer pricing regulations. *Id.* In order to prevent distorted tax revenues, the OECD Transfer Pricing Guidelines provides that profits from these transactions, which are not at arm's length, should be adjusted by treating the parties as if they were independent of each other. *See Transfer Pricing Guidelines for Multinational Enterprises and Tax Administration, supra* note 35. This is accomplished by comparing different conditions, including prices, made by related entities to those what those conditions would be if made by independent parties. *See id.* Then the profits of what would have been an arm's length transaction are calculated. *See id.*

[36] *See id.*

- address the tax challenges of the digital economy;[37]
- neutralize the effects of hybrid mismatch arrangements;[38]
- strengthen controlled foreign company rules;[39]
- limit base erosion via internet deductions and other financial payments;[40]
- counter harmful tax practices more effectively;[41]
- prevent treaty abuse;[42]
- prevent the artificial avoidance of permanent establishment status;[43]

---

[37] *See Subcommittee on Base Erosion and Profit Shifting Issues for Developing Countries*, UNITED NATIONS (last visited Nov. 23, 2017), http://www.un.org/esa/ffd/tax/BEPS_note.pdf. International Taxation principles and guideline have been developed through history, for this reason, the Subcommittee seeks to identify the complications that the new digital world and economic present to the historic international taxation principles. *Id.* Some of the areas the OECD will study include: the ability of a company to have a significant digital presence in the economy of another country without being liable to taxation due to the lack of nexus under current international rules, the attribution of value created from the generation of marketable location-relevant data through the use of digital products and services, the characterization of income derived from new business models, the application of related source rules, and how to ensure the effective collection of VAT/GST with respect to the cross-border supply of digital goods and services. *Id.*

[38] *Id.* at 8. Subcommittee proposes to develop a model treaty to neutralize the effect of different treatment of the same item of income or taxation regiment for different entities in different jurisdictions, reflecting their sovereign choices, which has led to double non-taxation. *Id.*

[39] *Id.* at 9. Strengthen the Controlled foreign company (CFC) rules, which apply when the resident of one country owns a significant interest in a foreign company, to counter Base Erosion and Profit-Shifting. *Id.*

[40] *Id.* at 10. Develop recommendations that use interest expenses and maximizing debt to prevent base erosion. *Id.*

[41] *Id.* at 11. To become more appealing to investors many States have developed harm taxation practices such as lowering tax rates, providing incentives, exempting certain forms of income or granting tax holidays. Therefore, the Subcommittee proposes to rehabilitate these practices using a holistic approach. *Id.*

[42] *Id.* at 12. The subcommittee plans to develop model treaty provisions and recommendations regarding the design of domestic rules to prevent the granting of treaty benefits inappropriate circumstances. *Id.* Treaty abuse includes a practice known as "treaty shopping" where a person obtains benefits of a treaty that they should not be entitled to. *Id.*

[43] *Id.* at 13. Develop and amend the definition with strict and clear guidance of Permanent Establishment, the point where an entity triggers taxation in a county because of its presence there, to prevent artificial avoidance. *Id.*

- assure that transfer pricing outcomes are in line with value creation;[44]
- require taxpayers to disclose their aggressive tax planning arrangements;[45]
- make dispute resolution mechanisms more effective;[46] and
- develop a multilateral instrument.[47]

Ultimately, base erosion and profit shifting have adverse implications on developing countries. The Subcommittee was created to minimize such negative effects by creating uniformity in how multinationals are taxed.

Yet, even with the current reform-oriented Managing Director, for the BWI the two urgently needed reforms and the urgently needed deeper transparency all seem unlikely. The neoliberal policies of the BWI for developing countries will most likely continue to favor the interests of developed countries.

---

[44] *Id.* at 13-5. The subcommittee is taking three actions in the areas of intangibles, Risk and Capital, and Other High-Risk Transaction to ensure that Multinational Enterprises are following the OEDC's Transfer Pricing Guidelines. *Id.* In other words, the subcommittee takes action to assure that the compensation given for a transaction within an MNE group should be equivalent to the price of an identical transaction between two unrelated parties. *Id.* at 17. Develop transfer pricing regulations that include a requirement that Multinational Enterprises to provide all relevant governments with needed information on their income, economic activity and taxes paid among countries. *Id.*

[45] *Id.* at 16. The work the Subcommittee proposes is a mandatory disclosure of aggressive or abusive transactions by using a modular design that allows country specific needs and risks. *Id.* One focus will be on international tax schemes, where they will explore using a wide definition of "tax benefit" in order to capture such transactions. *Id.*

[46] *Id.* at 15-16. The subcommittee explains the benefits of the actions taken thus:
This action seeks to gain a clearer picture of the impact of base erosion and profit shifting based on currently available studies and to identify what further data is required, and which methods should be employed in the future, to quantify the impacts of measures taken as a result of the action plan. This analysis will examine not only the tax impact of base erosion and profit shifting, and counter-measures, but also the broader impacts on a jurisdiction's economy and wealth
Id.

[47] *Id.* at 18. The Subcommittee seeks to develop a multilateral instrument to enable jurisdiction to implement its measures in the course of the work on Base Erosion Profit-Shifting and amend bilateral tax treaties.

The ultimate reason for lack of serious reform is that the core structure of the BWI gives the voice of developed countries much greater voting weight than the voice of the developing countries.

As an analogy, we might say that the BWI are like a corporation in which the developed countries constitute the majority shareholders who then control its board of directors. In turn, their control of the corporation is for their own benefit as the largest shareholders.

Without a deep reform of the core structures of the International Monetary Fund and the World Bank, developed countries will presumably continue to impose on the developed countries policies that will further open their economies to the benefit of controlling developed countries.

For that reason, the newly globalized world economy urgently needs a more democratic global regulatory financial architecture.

Deep reform of the core structures of the global financial architecture is now urgently needed to support socially and ecologically responsible development for both developed and developing nations. A few rich and powerful countries should no longer be allowed to financially dominate our newly globalized world economy across our now interconnected, resource-stressed, and small planet.

This book and future books from Pacem in Terris Press,
are available at:

www.amazon.com/books